Dallas Museum of Art

Daniel Barsotti

Dallas Museum of Art
SELECTED WORKS

by Dr. Anne R. Bromberg
Curator for Education

First Edition
Library of Congress Catalog Card Number 83-71457
ISBN 0-9609622-2-0 Hardback
ISBN 0-9609622-3-9 Paperback

Published and Edited by Robert V. Rozelle
Designed by James A. Ledbetter
Photography by David Wharton
Printed in Italy by Amilcare Pizzi, S.p.A., Milan

Dallas Museum of Art
1717 North Harwood
Dallas, Texas 75201

COVER
Claude Monet, *The Seine at Lavacourt,* 1880

FRONTISPIECE
Dallas Museum of Art, 1983

Table of Contents

Preface

The history of the Dallas Museum of Art parallels that of Dallas itself. Both were founded under less than ideal circumstances, the City without an abundance of natural resources, and the present Museum's antecedent as a small association of citizens whose love of art belied the absence of great art in the Dallas area at that time. Despite their tentative beginnings, the histories of both the Museum and the City have been characterized by dynamic periods of growth, interim periods of consolidation and renewal, and always by the active involvement of civic-minded people whose spirit of volunteerism, generosity, and resourceful dedication have long been recognized as the hallmarks of a unique community. In short, Dallas and its Art Museum have grown together.

Dallas Museum of Art, Selected Works has been published to commemorate the opening of the new Museum, a vibrant institution intended to serve all in the Dallas community. The *raison d'etre* of the Museum is therefore all the more meaningful in that its existence is due to a popular referendum approved by citizens in a 1979 bond election. There were extraordinary individual contributions, of course, but credit for the continuing evolution of the Museum and its emergence downtown belongs to the people of Dallas as a whole.

The purpose of this publication is to provide Museum visitors with an interesting and informative survey of the breadth and strengths of the City's art collections. It is hoped that the book will be used, and enjoyed, as an educational tool. In view of its expected application, the book's narrative descriptions have been authored, appropriately, by Dr. Anne R. Bromberg, DMA Curator for Education. Her insightful observations, broad knowledge of art history, and humanistic approach to such a comprehensive subject, should make this volume the useful tool for which it is intended. The task of assembling the publication, its textual and visual elements, into a readable and attractive whole has been ably conducted by Robert V. Rozelle, DMA Publisher and Editor.

On the occcasion of celebrating the new Museum, I would be remiss if I did not express on behalf of the community our excitement in opening such an elegantly conceived facility. Architect Edward Larrabee Barnes has designed a building that is both dramatic in scale and intimate in experience. Spacious, yet humane, formal but also flexible, the new Museum was consciously designed to receive our distinctive art collections and the people who visit to admire them. The integrity of a building is fully expressed only when there are people present, and we think visitors to the Dallas Museum of Art will appreciate the architectural environment as much as they enjoy viewing the art works housed within.

The Museum exists for the enjoyment and enrichment of the people of Dallas, so it is especially appropriate that its citizens regard this new facility as a gift to the City and the regional community of which it is a part. Both Dallas and the Museum have entered yet another phase of growth, in 1984, a new era of hopeful promise and continued civic involvement. As Dallas becomes ever more recognized as a city of national prominence, so also will the Dallas Museum of Art emerge as a widely recognized art institution of distinction. A city's stature is measured, in part, by the degree of art appreciation among its community. Both Dallas and the Museum, we believe, have good reason to be optimistic about their interrelated future together.

Harry S. Parker III
Director

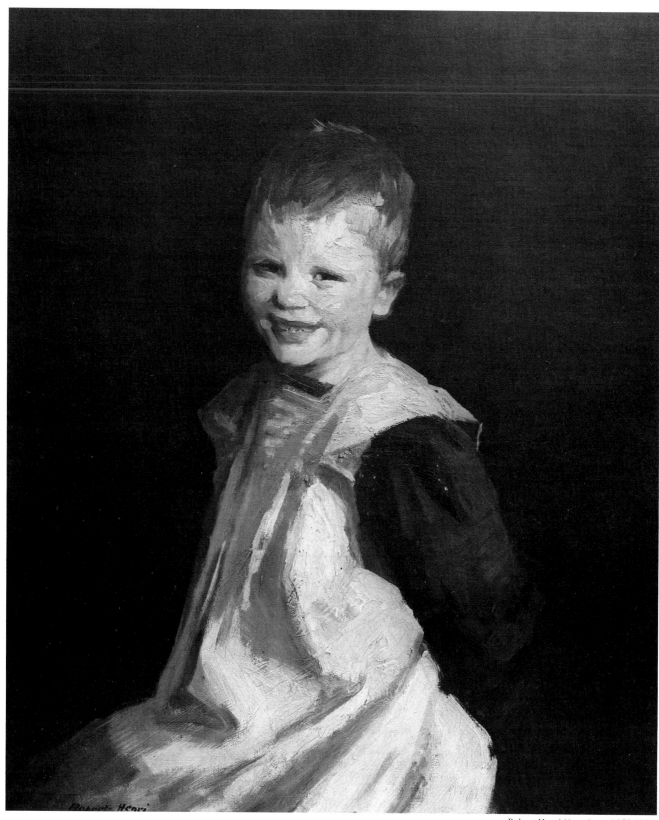

Robert Henri (American, 1865-1929)
DUTCH BOY LAUGHING
1907
oil on canvas
h: 32 in., w: 26 in.
Dallas Art Association purchase
1909.2

An Historical Perspective on the Collections

As with most museums, the history of collecting at the Dallas Museum of Art is a complicated record involving the personal tastes and commitments of individual directors and curators, the involvement of enlightened benefactors, changing philosophies of collecting weighed against the realities of funding and market opportunities, and just plain chance. Certain factors, however, distinguish the collection evolution in Dallas. Parallels can be drawn, for example, between the timing of the Museum's emergence in the 30s and 40s as a leading regional art center and the relatively late emergence of Dallas as a city of major econo-political importance.

Unlike some museums that have grown through the infusion of substantial acquisition endowments or the philanthropy of one or two primary patrons, the Dallas collection is built on broad community support, whether expressed in donations of art works or funds for individual purchases. Partially as a result, the Museum collection mirrors to a certain degree the collecting strengths and lacunae of the community. For example, there has never been a significant constituency for Old Master paintings in the Dallas private sector, and the Museum collection is also thin in this area, while the Museum's increasingly fine holdings of Impressionist, Post-Impressionist, and contemporary art reflect and benefit from dynamic private interest in these fields. In short, the Museum's collection, relatively speaking, is a youthful one that has grown through broad-based participation and is characterized by definite pools of strength linked by narrower art historical threads. The history of growth has been a happy partnership between professional expertise and community support. While a full study of this history is needed to supplement Jerry Bywaters' enlightening *Seventy-Five Years of Art in Dallas* (1978), it seems appropriate upon the occasion of publishing an expanded and revised survey of the collections to review some of its highlights.

The early years of collecting by the Dallas Art Association, parent body of the present Museum, were characterized by noble efforts backed by limited resources. In addition to organizing exhibitions and educational programs, the Association sought to create a permanent collection through regular purchases and gifts.

Emphasis was directed primarily at recent American art, and with the help of contributions, dues, and fund raising the Association was able to make a number of purchases of lasting importance, including Childe Hassam's *September Moonrise,* bought in 1903, and Robert Henri's *Dutch Boy Laughing,* acquired in 1909.

Operated by private citizens and eventually located in a Fine Arts building on the State Fair grounds, the Dallas Art Association championed a spirit of collecting and art patronage through the first three decades of our century. A major boost to these efforts came in 1925 with the establishment by Mrs. S.I. Munger of a $50,000 endowment for acquisitions, the first such fund of its kind. Some of the early purchases from the Munger Fund, still an important acquisition resource, include Emil Carlsen's *Study in Grey* (bought in 1926) and Claude Monet's *The Seine at Lavacourt,* obtained in 1938.

With the growth of the Association's collection and activities and the eventual hiring of a professional director, the need became apparent for a proper art museum. This void was finally filled in 1936 by the construction in Fair Park of the Dallas Museum of Fine Arts as part of an architectural complex planned for the State Centennial celebration. Thus was inaugurated a new era of collection consciousness that is now shifting once again with the downtown opening in 1984 of the new Dallas Museum of Art.

Progress at first was not rapid, but helping make up for rather fitful growth was the placement on long-term loan (a designation recently changed to "promised gift") of the Hoblitzelle Foundation's collection of Old Master paintings. Formed in Paris and Lima, Peru, and brought into this country by a member of the Hoblitzelle family, this collection has long provided the backbone of the Museum's Old Master holdings, and includes such fine paintings as Paolini's *Bacchic Concert* and Michael Sweert's *Portrait of a Young Officer.*

Under the twenty-one year directorship (1943-64) of Jerry Bywaters, an artist himself and a specialist in Southwestern and Mexican art, the growth of regional representation received special consideration, while contemporary American art at-large was the principle collecting goal, due in part to the theory that limited funds could be used to greatest effect in contemporary art. Works were acquired, for example, by Alexandre Hogue, Ernest Blumenschein, Wiliam Zorach, George Grosz, Thomas Hart Benton, George Bellows, Charles Burchfield, Edward Hopper, and Reginald Marsh, either by purchase or gift. A bequest from Joel T. Howard of 36 paintings strongly benefited the holdings of late 19th and early 20th century American art, and leading avant-garde trends were given representation through gifts of works by Alexander Calder *(Flower,* 1949) and Jackson Pollock *(Cathedral,* 1947) and the commission of a large mural by Rufino Tamayo *(Man,* 1953). In 1960 the McDermott Fund, established by Eugene and Margaret McDermott, joined the Munger Fund in the ranks of acquisition endowments and also marked one of the earliest in a long series of major acts of generosity toward the Museum by this remarkable couple. The McDermott Fund has been used for a diverse variety of works, from sculptures by Degas and David Smith to Pre-Columbian, Japanese, and Indonesian objects.

It was during this period, in 1956, that a civic group interested in promoting greater appreciation of contemporary art founded the Society for Contemporary Arts, later renamed the Dallas Museum of Contemporary Art. Under the able directorship of Douglas MacAgy, this institution not only carried on an ambitious exhibition program but also began assembling a collection of key works of 20th century art, including major examples by Redon, Matisse, Bacon, and Nicholson and the much loved *Watch* and *Razor* by Gerald Murphy. Another milestone in the history of the Museum was passed in 1962 when the Museum of Contemporary Art merged with the Museum of Fine Arts and, simultaneously, the Foundation for the Arts was formed as a holding agency for the collection of the former DMCA and as a body able to solicit funds and make acquisitions to be placed at the disposal of the Museum. Soon after these major steps, Merrill Rueppel succeeded Jerry Bywaters as director.

Efforts under the Rueppel administration often focused on broadening the collection into areas previously represented only minimally or not at all, and numerous fine acquisitions were made, for example, in Pre-Columbian and ancient art and in Oriental painting. Emphasis was also placed on continued expansion of the contemporary collection, which was emerging as one of the best in the Southwest. Added to the collection at this time were important paintings by Jim Dine, Arshile Gorky, Franz Kline, Adolphe Gottlieb, and Robert Motherwell, and sculptures by Henry Moore, Jean Arp, and Barbara Hepworth. Playing increasingly vital roles in the realm of acquisitions were several families, such as the Meadows, Clarks, Greens, Edward Marcuses and Stanley Marcuses, all of whom have left an indelible mark on the Museum. A more distant source of support, resulting in a series of gifts of earlier European paintings and sculptures, came from New York and foundations headed by Josephine Bay and Col. C. Michael Paul. Of special distinction at this time and of particular long-range impact were the purchases of several complete collections of Pre-Columbian and African art, giving the Museum pre-eminence in these fields: the Stillman Collection of Congo sculpture presented by Mr. and Mrs. Eugene McDermott in 1969; the Schindler Collection of African art, a gift of the McDermott Foundation (1975); and the Nora and John Wise Collection of ancient American art, presented by Mrs. Eugene McDermott, Mr. and Mrs. Algur H. Meadows, Mr. and Mrs. John D. Murchison, and Mr. and Mrs. Jake L. Hamon (1976).

By 1973 Harry S. Parker, III, had assumed the reins of directorship. He has led the Museum through a period of rapidly escalating art prices and the stepped-up solicitation of private funds to meet this challenge, as well as the planning of a new building to provide superior facilities for collection care, display, and expansion. A particularly salutary event occurred in 1977 with the bequest from Mrs. John B. O'Hara to the Foundation for the Arts of a $4.5 million purchase fund, by far the Museum's largest, to be used for 18th and 19th century art. Among other fine works purchased with this fund have been Courbet's *Fox in the Snow,* Daumier's *Outside the Print-Seller's Shop,* and Vernet's *Mountain Landscape with Approaching Storm.*

In recent years, other major strides have been made with the receipt of 38 paintings and sculptures from the Meadows Foundation Collection of Impressionist and modern masters, eight outstanding works by Léger and Mondrian from the Clark Foundation, the monumental *Icebergs* by Frederic Church from an anonymous donor, and two important paintings, a Modigliani and a Sargent, from the Leland Fikes Foundation. In preparation for the new building an ambitious program of commissioned sculptures for specific locations was undertaken, with commissions awarded to Claes Oldenburg, Ellsworth Kelly, Richard Fleischner, and Scott Burton. Noteworthy also are the accomplishments made through the Hamon Fund for contemporary prints and the Camp Fund, applied generally in the primitive or Pre-Columbian fields, while the Edward S. Marcus Fund has made possible several important purchases of modern sculpture.

Many and varied have been the sources feeding the growth of the Dallas Museum, and on the eve of dedicating a handsome new facility the Museum can look back proudly over an interesting history of collecting. The art works assembled trace a broad span of man's creativity, with several areas of present and emerging strength. There remains much to be accomplished, and the new Museum offers a special challenge for further collection development, but the continued tradition in Dallas of partnership between professional expertise and private benefaction bodes well for meeting that challenge.

Dr. Steven A Nash
Assistant Director/Chief Curator
1983

Paul Sérusier (French, 1983-1927)
CELTIC TALE
1894
oil on canvas
h: 43⅜ in., w: 39¾ in.
Foundation for the Arts Collection,
gift of Mr. and Mrs. Frederick M. Mayer
1983.52.FA

138.
Aristide Maillol
FLORA

51.
Ibo
STANDING FEMALE FIGURE

Introduction

The purpose of this book is to offer an overview of the Dallas Museum of Art's collections, on the occasion of their installation in the new Museum facility. Many new acquisitions are on view in the galleries, as well as works for which previously there was no display space. Examples of contemporary sculpture have been commissioned to complement the architecture of the new building. The presentation of the Museum's art is therefore considerably different from the exhibits in the old building. This volume is intended to highlight major works in the Museum's diverse art collections and to make the Museum goer's visit more knowledgeable and more enjoyable.

The format of the book follows, in general, the layout of the Museum's galleries, beginning with the Non-Western collections on the third level. In this area are Pre-Columbian, African, Indonesian, Oceanic, American Indian, Hispanic-American, Oriental and Ancient Mediterranean art. These collections are described in chapters 1 through 8. The building's intermediate level is devoted to European and American art through the Early Modern period, which is discussed in chapters 9 through 13. On the ground level is Contemporary Art, some examples of which are also on display in the Museum's main corridor and in the Sculpture Garden. These works are illustrated in the chapters on Contemporary American Art. The Museum also includes areas devoted to Prints, Drawings and Photographs and to the Textile collection, which are described in the last two chapters of the book.

While this volume cannot be considered a true guide to the art in the Museum, as it illustrates and describes only selected high points of the collections, it does attempt to convey the quality of the art to be found at DMA and to give an historical or cultural context for the works. The text was written by the Curator For Education, in part because of the educational role the Museum is expected to play in the Dallas community.

Although the Museum is not strong in some areas of European art, it has, in compensation, an international collection. One of the DMA's major attributes is the opportunity it offers to compare art from widely different traditions. The particular strengths of the Museum in Ethnic and in Contemporary art emphasize the importance of media in art and the way artists deal with problems of technique and craftsmanship.

One appeal of the Dallas Museum of Art is the presence of the unexpected. Ancient Pre-Columbian gold work or rare textiles may be compared with Scott Burton's monolithic granite settee or Claes Oldenburg's great Pop Art tent stake. Traditional American portraits and landscapes are in close proximity to the explosive work of the American Abstract Expressionists. A modern wood sculpture recalls the aesthetics of African ritual wood carvings. Impressionist scenes contrast with the presentation of nature in Japanese painting. One of the very rare 4th century Greek marble statues represents the beginning of classical and archetypal sculpture, a tradition continued much later in Aristide Maillol's *Flora,* and in Constantin Brancusi's abstract work, *Beginning of the World.*

Humanism is the keynote of the Museum's collections, and the great variety of human creativity is the continuing theme of this book. Art is not only man-made, it is the mirror that men everywhere hold up to their deepest selves. The large mural painting by the Mexican artist Rufino Tamayo, for years one of the Museum's most popular works, expresses this difficult achievement: a symbolic figure of mankind struggles out of a dark abyss towards a heaven lit with comets and stars.

Dallas Museum of Art, Selected Works would not have been possible without the help and goodwill of a number of people on the staff of the Museum or otherwise associated with it. Since the book is a joint effort in honor of the new Museum facility, first thanks should go to the Director, Harry S. Parker III, and to the members of the Board of Trustees, whose vision and devoted efforts made the new building possible. In the actual writing of the book I would like to acknowledge the extremely generous help, which included ideas, expertise and useful criticism, contributed by the Curatorial Department: Dr. Steven Nash, Assistant Director and Chief Curator; John Lunsford,

Senior Curator; Sue Graze, Curator for Contemporary Art; and Carol Robbins, Associate Curator. They are responsible for the choice of illustrations in the book, but in a far deeper sense, the art displayed at the Museum is their chief concern. I can only hope I have done justice to their scholarly commitment to the collections.

Invaluable research was contributed by Marie Canaves, the 1982/83 McDermott Graduate Intern in Education. The photographs in the book owe a great deal to the hard work of David Wharton, Museum Photographer, and to Ann Fricke, Assistant Registrar. Robert V. Rozelle, Publisher/Publicity Director, has been responsible for overseeing the entire project, including production and printing. James Ledbetter, the designer of the book, has approached the Museum's collections with his usual, understanding sensitivity. Melissa Berry, Administrative Assistant in the Education Department, had the responsibility for the typescript at every stage of its development, which was an exacting and laborious operation. I am greatly indebted to the hard work and enthusiasm of all these people, who have participated in this project, and have ensured it would be ready in time for the opening of the new Dallas Museum of Art.

Dr. Anne R. Bromberg
Curator For Education

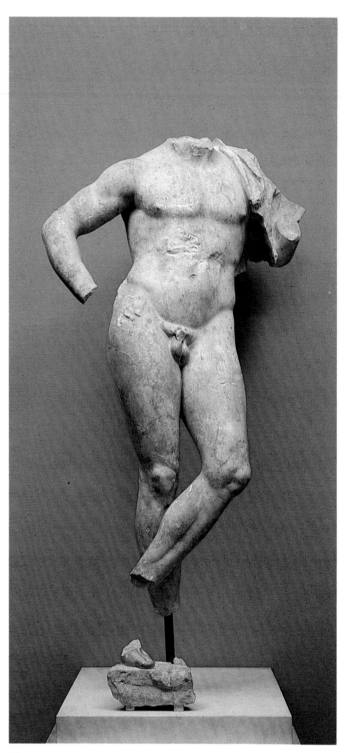

97.
Greek
FIGURE OF A YOUNG MAN
FROM A FUNERARY RELIEF

10

Collections of the
Dallas Museum of Art

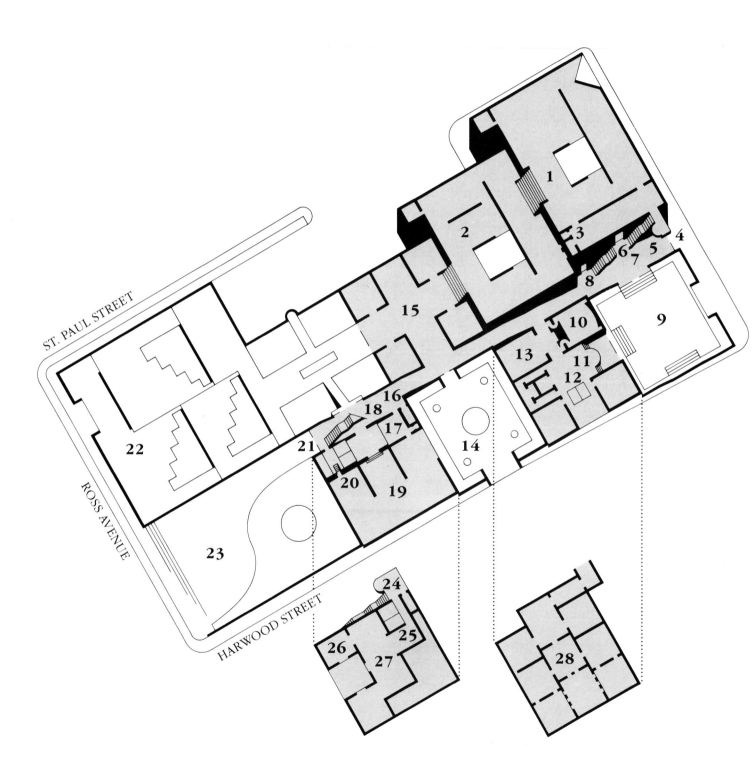

1 Pre-Columbian, Ethnic, Oriental & Ancient Mediterranean Galleries

2 Traditional European & American Galleries

3 Elevator

4 Parking lot entrance

5 Libraries entrance

6 Museum Offices

7 Auditorium entrance, Restrooms

8 Entrance to Study Gallery for Prints, Drawings, Textiles & Photographs
Elevator, Lockers, Telephones & Information Desk

9 Education Courtyard

10 Orientation Theater

11 Education Wing

12 Restrooms

13 Museum Shops

14 Flora Street Entrance Courtyard

15 Contemporary Galleries

16 Restaurant Elevators

17 Handicapped Access to Temporary Exhibition Galleries

18 Information Desk

19 Temporary Exhibition Galleries

20 Restrooms, Lockers & Telephones

21 Ross Avenue Entrance

22 Sculpture Garden

23 Plaza

24 Restaurant Elevator

25 Restaurant Restrooms

26 Founders Room

27 Gallery Buffet Restaurant

28 Expansion Galleries

12.

I.

Pre-Columbian Middle American Art

When the Spanish first came to the Americas, in the wake of Columbus' discovery of the New World, they found various Indian groups, all of a distant East Asiatic descent, and some the creators of remarkably complex civilizations. In 1519 Hernán Cortés and a small band of Spanish soldiers rode inland from the coast of Mexico — on the first horses in the New World since prehistoric times — to find the great Aztec capital of Tenochtitlan and, by 1521, to conquer it. They were dazzled by the exotic wealth of the Aztec kingdom, but they were also horrified by religious and cultural practices, such as human sacrifice and ritual cannibalism, which they considered pagan. In later years the Spanish ruled a vast American empire, stretching from California and New Mexico to the tip of South America, all of which had been converted to the Spanish Catholic faith.

But the native Indian civilization did not altogether disappear, even though the Spanish rulers destroyed many art works and written documents. A few of the lavish art works of the ancient Mexican and Maya people were carried back to Spain; others remained in the tombs, sacred caches or abandoned temples where they had been placed originally, until they were rediscovered by modern archaeologists. Also, many Pre-Spanish religious practices and beliefs survived among the native population.

Since the 19th century, archaeological and scholarly research, as well as the patriotic interest of Latin Americans in their past, has led to a striking re-evaluation of the art of these Indian kingdoms. They are now seen to have produced very sophisticated art styles comparable to the ancient cultures of Egypt, Greece, India or China. Since such writings as have survived from these societies are still being slowly interpreted, there is less precise knowledge of the cultural context of art works than one would find in the historically well-known societies of Eurasia, but in technical skill, rich religious symbolism and aesthetic power Pre-Columbian art is fully comparable to Old Kingdom Egypt or Bronze Age China.

Apparently these New World civilizations developed largely independently of Eurasia. Great architecture, cities and religious centers, a class system, writing, intellectual knowledge of mathematics and astronomy, complex agricultural methods: all of these elements developed in the area now called Middle America. From a heartland in central and southern Mexico, Guatemala, Belize, Honduras and El Salvador, cultural influences spread both north and south on the American continents. Probably the various peoples living in this area shared generally similar religious ideas, traded with each other, fought, and exchanged diplomatic relations. Art works from Middle America seem to share common values of ritual and power.

1.

2.

1.
JOINED PAIR OF FIGURES
Tlatilco, 1150-550 B.C.
Mexico:Valley of Mexico, Tlatilco
ceramic
h: 15 3/8 in., w: 12 3/8 in.
Gift of Mr. and Mrs. Eugene McDermott
and the McDermott Foundation
and Mr. and Mrs. Algur H. Meadows
and the Meadows Foundation, Incorporated
1973.72

The high civilizations of Middle America grew up on a basis of village life. After the domestication of corn and other crops, which made possible larger populations, a great number of art works were made which emphasized magic, fertility and local shamanic practices. Such ritual artifacts may be found in other village societies around the world. Pre-Columbian clay figurines of this sort were probably offerings or amulets, and reflect the rich ceremonial life of village people. Dancers, musicians, acrobats, animals and female fertility figures are rendered with great liveliness and charm.

The joined figures of this work from the site of Tlatilco may be ritual dancers; they also reflect the motif of twins, which was of important mythic significance in Middle America. The figurine, like many of the Tlatilco finds, is an advanced type of ceramic: it is hollow, with a hard body and a finely finished surface. Even at this relatively early stage, Mexican potters show a refined technique and a boldly stylized form, which is all the more remarkable because the craftsmen had neither the potter's wheel nor kilns. Pre-Columbian ceramics are hand-made or mold-made and were fired in the open.

2.
COLOSSAL AXE: DEITY FIGURE
Attributed to the Carver of the Kunz Axe
Olmec, 1150-550 B.C.
Mexico: Tabasco
stone
h: 10 3/8 in., w: 5 3/4 in., d: 4 11/16 in.
Gift of Mr. and Mrs. Eugene McDermott
and the McDermott Foundation
and Mr. and Mrs. Algur H. Meadows
and the Meadows Foundation, Incorporated
1973.29

By 1200 B.C. the various settled cultures of Middle America had fairly large populations and rich art styles. The first people who seem to have developed a more complex level of social organization were the Olmec, who lived primarily in the coastal area of Mexico around Veracruz. For the first time one finds large-scale temples, evidence for a stratified society, trade in luxury items like jadeite or obsidian. The Olmec may also have been connected with the origins of the Middle American pantheon of gods and the first form of the religious calendar system, with its interlocking cycles of time.

As there is little writing from Olmec sites, Olmec influence on religious imagery is debatable. Perhaps Olmec deity figures, like this impressive stone axe, may represent an early vision of what would later become the great Middle American gods of rain, fertility, sacrifice, death, and the Underworld. Most Middle American gods occur in different forms, representing day and night, earthly life and death, or the four directional points symbolized by different colors. Plant, sky and animal imagery is attached to each incarnation of a god or goddess. The stark power of the sculpture, with its snarling, animal-like features, may be related to rain and fertility; it also has elements of the jaguar deity and of death. In Pre-Columbian religion, life and death form a continuum, as the sun rises and sets every day, and this unity is often referred to in artistic imagery.

Impressive works like this, which took endless hours of labor to carve by the simplest means of wet sand, twisted cords and bamboo drill, were designed to be buried forever in caches or tombs. Art served the ends of magic and religion and had an endless immortal life in the spirit world. Often, the carved figures or ornamental celts of precious stone were consecrated by the Olmec in a group, like a miniature Stonehenge.

4.

3.

3.
MASK
Olmec, 800-400 B.C.
Mexico: Veracruz, Arroyo Pesquero
jadeite
h: 7 1/8 in., w: 6 9/16 in., d: 4 in.
Gift of Mr. and Mrs. Eugene McDermott
and the McDermott Foundation
and Mr. and Mrs. Algur H. Meadows
and the Meadows Foundation, Incorporated
1973.17

Just as Olmec ritual seems to have displayed an identity of life and death, sun and darkness, so there was an interplay between the power of a king or noble in life and after death. A jadeite mask like this one might, perhaps, have been worn by a great ruler during his lifetime, when he was taking upon himself the role of god or spirit. It would then have been buried with

him when he died, to crystallize his power forever, like Egyptian or Chinese tomb figures.

While there is no direct evidence for the way kings were considered in this early historical period, it seems likely that they were thought to belong to the supernatural realm and that their distinguished lineage connected them with mythic beings. Their power was more than this world.

The superb, if enigmatic, clarity of this Olmec mask — its pure and simple form, which yet hints of snarling animal power — establishes an identity between human and divine, the actual person of the ruler and the god he impersonates.

18

5.

4.
SEATED MAN
Olmec, 800-500 B.C.
Mexico: Puebla
serpentine, cinnabar
h: 7 3/32 in., w: 5 3/8 in., d: 3 1/16 in.
Gift of Mr. and Mrs. Eugene McDermott,
the Roberta Coke Camp Fund,
and the Art Museum League Fund
1983.50

A similar mastery of stone carving may be seen in the Olmec *Seated Figure of a Man,* a work in dark green serpentine. Despite the small size of the piece, the figure emanates an air of effortless authority and probably represents the portrait of an historical Olmec ruler. The subtle asymmetry of the man's seated pose, as well as the features of his face, heavy with the weight of experience and power, may imply a real person within the formalized dignity of the image. The fluid grace of line in the sculpture, allied to the suave smoothness of the green stone, has an harmonious resonance, which is highlighted by the cinnabar pigment used to emphasize facial features and body modelling. Such a work, which possibly formed part of a sacred cache, weds a marvelous technical skill to a ritual purpose, creating a sculpture of powerful simplicity and glowing intensity.

19

5.
SEATED MAN AND WOMAN
Jalisco, Ameca Gray Type, 100 B.C.-A.D.250
Mexico: Jalisco
ceramic
h: 16 1/16 in., w: 18 5/8 in.
Gift of Mr. and Mrs. Eugene McDermott
and the McDermott Foundation
and Mr. and Mrs. Algur H. Meadows
and the Meadows Foundation, Incorporated
1973.58

In Western Mexico the tradition of the village cultures lasted up to the Spanish conquest. Here, religious experience was still that of the local magician, or shaman, who could communicate with the spirit world in a state of trance and cure people's illnesses. The many fine ceramic figures found in West Mexican shaft tombs probably reflect this kind of shamanic magic, rather than the highly organized ceremonial rituals of the various Classic Period societies in Mexico. The style and technique of the ceramics is also close to the earlier village traditions.

From the state of Jalisco comes this figure of a seated man and woman. On the human side, the couple represents marriage and fertility, and they are depicted with the immediate warmth characteristic of West Mexican work. Yet their wonderfully fluid gestures may reflect the magical gestures of shamanic rites. Such works may have been offerings, or memorials of shamanic ceremonies, especially funerary ceremonies. The effortless freedom of the clay modelling, uniting the two figures in one continuous curving line, and the sensuous polished surface of the piece show the artistic mastery of Mexican potters.

6.
JAR WITH PARROT MAN MOTIF
Casas Grandes (Ramos Polychrome Type), A.D.1060-1340
Mexico: Chihuahua
ceramic, paint
h: 6 in., dia: 7 7/16 in.
Dallas Museum of Fine Arts purchase
1980.15

The West Mexican ceramic styles are rather on the fringes of the high civilizations of Middle America, but there are traces of Middle American influence even farther afield — all the way north to the Pueblo cultures of the Mogollon and Anasazi in the American Southwest, where there are distant echoes of Mexican ceremonial ball courts and large-scale architecture. In northern Mexico, the site of Casas Grandes included multi-story buildings, like the Pueblo buildings in the Southwest, and an art style somewhere in between the Valley of Mexico and prehistoric Pueblo Indian style. The figure of a feathered serpent on this bowl relates to the Mexican god/hero Quetzalcoatl — Feathered Serpent — while the flamboyant diagonal pattern of the bowl, and its wheeling forms, are closer to Pueblo pottery. The striking image of the running bird-man may also be some local version of Mexican mythology.

6.

7.

7.
FACE EFFIGY
Teotihuacan, A.D.200-400
Mexico
stone
h: 12 5/8 in., w: 11 1/8 in.
Gift of Mr. and Mrs. Eugene McDermott
and the McDermott Foundation
and Mr. and Mrs. Algur H. Meadows
and the Meadows Foundation, Incorporated
1973.49

In the Classic Period of Middle American history, between about 200 and 800 A.D., several areas reached a height of political power and artistic creativity. The urban ceremonial center of Teotihuacan, north of Mexico City, was probably the center of a large and powerful state, whose rulers could command the manpower to construct a great complex of temples, shrines, palaces and shops. The sculptural style of Teotihuacan is stern and severe, perhaps indicating the warlike side of Teotihuacan society. A stone effigy like this one would have been buried with a high-ranking person. The stylized force of its brutally simplified forms is in great contrast with the suave Olmec mask from Arroyo Pesquero, which suggested a real person as much as supernatural power.

8b.

8a.

9.

8.a
SEATED MAN WITH SHOULDER TABS
Veracruz Monumental Sculpture, A.D.600-900
Mexico: Veracruz
ceramic
h: 26 3/4 in., w: 21 in., d: 21 1/16 in.
1976.W5

8.b
SEATED MAN WITH HANDS ON KNEES
Veracruz Monumental Sculpture, A.D.600-900
Mexico: Veracruz
ceramic
h: 26 3/8 in., w: 19 3/16 in., d: 18 13/16 in.
1976.W4

9.
SEATED MAN EXAMINING WOUNDS
Veracruz Monumental Sculpture, A.D.600-900
Mexico: Veracruz
ceramic
h: 29 9/16 in., w: 19 1/16 in., d: 19 5/8 in.
1976.W3

The Nora and John Wise Collection,
gift of Mr. and Mrs. Jake L. Hamon,
the Eugene McDermott Family,
Mr. and Mrs. Algur H. Meadows
and the Meadows Foundation,
and Mr. and Mrs. John D. Murchison

Even more different from the stark style of Teotihuacan is the Museum's group of Classic Period statues from Veracruz. Much Middle American art is ritual in both purpose and appearance, but these almost life-size clay figures combine a vibrant lifelike effect with ceremonial meaning. Two of the seated figures appear to be triumphant chieftains, handsomely dressed and full of superb self-confidence. The third figure in the group is a naked, wounded man, slumped in pain and despair. He is probably about to become a sacrificial offering, as captives were often sacrificed in ancient Mexico. The dynamic vigor of these figures suggests an actual historical event, such as a conquest, but the whole group was probably intended as a ritual offering — demonstrating once again the implied unity of life and death, victory and sacrifice, in Middle American religion. Simply as an example of the technical difficulty of large clay sculpture these figures are very impressive, but their evocative human character and expressive power make them among the most striking of Pre-Columbian art works.

10.
CYLINDER VASE
Maya, A.D.600-900
Mexico: Campeche or Yucatan
ceramic
h: 9 in., max. dia: 7 1/8 in.
Gift of Mr. and Mrs. Eugene McDermott
and the McDermott Foundation
and Mr. and Mrs. Algur H. Meadows
and the Meadows Foundation, Incorporated
1973.33

Some of the most attractive and aesthetically appeal-ing art of the Classic Period comes from the Maya kingdoms in Yucatan, Guatemala, Belize and north-ern Honduras. Although the Maya shared many of the cultural traits of the rest of Middle America, they had their own very marked interests, including a greater development of hieroglyphic writing and calendrical systems and astronomy than other Pre-Columbian people. Their art is very distinctive, too, with much over-all patterning and a dynamic linear style. The bravura elegance of Maya art transcends any difficul-ties in interpreting the dense religious symbolism which is its subject matter.

The vital Maya line is apparent in the carving of this incised vase. An orchestral interplay of ornamental lines makes the vase highly decorative, but does not obscure the symbolic subject, in which a distinguished ruler/ancestor appears before a Maya divinity. The vase is a statement of magical status and power, as well as a luxuriant upper class art work.

11.
FEMALE DIGNITARY HOLDING SCEPTER
Maya, A.D.700-750
Mexico
limestone, plaster, traces of paint
h: 86 3/4 in., w: 30 1/4 in., d: 4 3/4 in.
Foundation for the Arts Collection,
gift of Mr. and Mrs. James H. Clark
1968.39.FA

The figures on the incised cylinder vase are carefully depicted in ceremonial dress and with appropriate attributes. This concentration on the trappings of lineage, divinity and power runs throughout Maya art. On this relief panel a very high-ranking Maya woman, who appears to be both princess and priestess, is garbed in a precious feather headdress, rich robes and jade

ornaments. The scepter she holds is topped by a god figure. She is an actual, historical personage, yet also a symbolization of the Maya nobility's contacts with a divine realm. The lavish patterning of the flat relief surface, as well as the symbolic colors with which the panel was once painted, create an image of hier-atic power. Moreover, the glyphs on the relief both explain the woman's status and form part of the rich decorative pattern. Writing is an integral part of Maya aesthetics.

10.

11.

12. *illustration on page 14*
ECCENTRIC FLINT: DESCENDING EARTH MONSTER
WITH HUMAN FIGURES ON ITS BACK
Maya, A.D. 650-800
Guatemala: Northern Petén
flint
h: 9 25/32 in., 1: 16 3/16 in. d: 21/32 in.
The Eugene and Margaret McDermott Fund
in honor of Mrs. Alex Spence
1983.45. McD

In the great Maya religious centers, offerings which were placed in shrines, buried in sacred caches, or left with the dead, were often different in character from the more monumental art styles. For instance, the odd shapes found in natural pieces of flint stone seem to have suggested the possibility of making magic objects from them, capitalizing on the easily worked character of flint and its sharp brilliance when chipped. One of the major works in the Museum's Pre-Columbian collection is a complex flint, which to an extreme degree presents the glittering linear elegance admired by the Maya. A work so fragile and intricate may well have been part of a ruler's regalia, to be buried after his death.

The flint sculpture is a tour de force of imagery. In overall form it is a double-headed dragon-like monster, familiar from other Maya works. Here, the monster appears to be diving down into the Underworld, with several divine or mythic images represented upon his back. The sharp and undulating lines of the flint suggest this plunging movement. The sophisticated ability of Maya artists to make visual puns is apparent in the fact that one of the heads on the monster's back actually forms the hand gesture of the major god figure, while the monster's clawed foot is yet another human head. Each of the heads which form part of the design has distinctive Maya features and headdress. While much Maya art is notable for this kind of packed iconographic detail, the DMA flint carving is a truly bravura play with traditional imagery, turning even irregularities in the flint into a jewelled brilliance of line and form.

13.

13.
HEAD OF THE RAIN GOD, TLALOC
Mixtec, A.D.1300-1500
Mexico: Oaxaca, Teotitlán del Camino
polychrome ceramic
h: 51 in., w: 41 in., d: 46 in.
Gift of Mr. and Mrs. Stanley Marcus
in memory of Mary Freiberg
1967.5

One of the oldest and most important of the Middle American gods was the rain deity Tlaloc. Farming people, who are completely dependent on the powers of nature, are vitally aware of the dangers of flood and drought: the dread powers that Tlaloc controlled. This powerful image of Tlaloc, made by the Mixtec people of Oaxaca, is a monumental clay sculpture of strange and forbidding appearance. A range of religious motifs, all symbolizing rain, make up the giant head: the long teeth symbolized falling water; the snakes on ears and eyebrows meant thunder; the great round eyes were painted blue for pools of water; the projection on the nose indicated Quetzalcoatl, in his guise as the planet Venus. Beyond the meaning of individual details, however, is the expressive force of the image, which suggests the violence, both beneficent and destructive, of a tropical thunderstorm.

Like the group of Classic Period Veracruz figures, the head of Tlaloc formed part of a shrine, probably in a cave. Here, in darkness and dripping water, the spirit of rain itself could overawe his worshippers.

14.
PECTORAL MASKETTE
Mixtec, A.D.1450-1500
Mexico
gold
h: 3 1/2 in., w: 3 5/8 in., d: 1 5/8 in.
The Nora and John Wise Collection,
gift of Mr. and Mrs. Jake L. Hamon,
the Eugene McDermott Family,
Mr. and Mrs. Algur H. Meadows
and the Meadows Foundation,
and Mr. and Mrs. John D. Murchison
1976.W1

Although gold-working was common from an early time in far Central and South America, it was hardly used in Middle America until a late period. The Mixtec were particularly adept at cast gold work, like this pectoral ornament in the shape of a mask. The recurrent importance of masks in Pre-Columbian art indicates the very elaborate ceremonies of impersonation, which are known from Spanish sources. Most of the equipment of these rituals has long since disappeared, but it once was a central part of people's lives.

14.

15.⟩

15.
MASK, POSSIBLY OF TLALOC
Aztec Period, A.D.1485-1519
Mexico
wood, turquoise, spondylus shell, lignite, resin
h: 7 11/16 in., w: 6 5/16 in., d: 3 5/8 in.
The Roberta Coke Camp Fund
1979.2

An even more dazzling example of ceremonial disguise may be seen in this Aztec mask, made of wood covered with a turquoise and shell inlay. Only a handful of such masks has survived, making this one of the Museum's most precious possessions. The extraordinary subtlety of the inlay, with its shifting tones and overall blue pigment, is yet another example of the sophisticated art possible with very simple tools, none of them made of metal.

While the mask may from time to time have been worn by ceremonial impersonators, taking part in the elaborate round of cyclical rites carried on in the Aztec capital, it may also have been used to decorate images of the gods. There is a very close interconnection in ancient Mexican art between a human disguised as a spirit or divinity, the statue of a divinity, and the actual divine being. The line between human and divine, or this life and a supernatural realm, was often blurred, or thought to be crossed by magic means.

It is very possible that this mask also represents the rain god, Tlaloc, which would explain the use of the blue color of water and the staring, hypnotic force of the image. Children were sacrificed to Tlaloc, to bring good crops in the fields: he is a god of terror and death, as well as life.

16.
XIPE IMPERSONATOR
Aztec, A.D.1400-1521
Mexico: Mexico City Area
volcanic stone, shell
h: 27 1/2 in., w: 11 in.
Gift of Mr. and Mrs. Eugene McDermott
and the McDermott Foundation
and Mr. and Mrs. Algur H. Meadows
and the Meadows Foundation, Incorporated
1973.65

Sacrifice is a central concept in Middle American religion. Blood was the food of gods and offerings of the living to death could insure continued life-giving crops in the fields. During the period of the Aztec empire, which was notable for wide-spread warfare and a spirit of militarism, this cult of human sacrifice reached a peak.

To Xipe Totec, god of springtime, victims were sacrificed by having their hearts torn from their breast. Priests and other celebrants then dressed in the skins of the victims. This stone figure shows a man dressed in the flayed skin of the victim. Its harsh power is typical of Aztec style. To the ancient Mexicans, the very gods had at times, like Quetzalcoatl, sacrificed themselves to bring about a new era of the world. The ritual sacrifice of victims was a magic means of carrying on the cycle of time and insuring that rebirth would follow death, as the crops spring up anew in the fields each year, or the sun is reborn, after its nightly death, each morning.

16.

II.

Pre-Columbian Central and South American Art

Soon after Cortés' conquest of Mexico, Spanish explorers of the New World led their armies to Peru. Here, too, the conquistadors found a rich civilization in the Inca Empire. Pizarro and his soldiers found palaces with walls covered in gold and statues of solid gold and silver. Cuzco, the Inca capital, seemed like a dream city of barbaric splendor come true. However, the highly centralized Inca kingdom was a very late development in the history of the Andes Mountains region; it had dominated Peru for less than a century when the Spanish arrived. For millennia before the Inca, Peruvian societies had developed along the river valleys that made the desert coastland of Peru habitable, and in the highlands of the Andes.

As in Mexico, the domestication of crops led to settled villages, though the ancient Peruvians also depended heavily on sea life. These native Indian societies never developed writing, and large-scale architecture or sculpture was less important here than in Middle America.

On the other hand, the Andean peoples were superb craftsmen: their complex textile techniques, elaborate ceramics and elegant gold work are the equal of similar work anywhere in the world.

Interpreting this ancient Andean art is difficult, due to the lack of written sources. Presumably much of the imagery, including birds, felines, sea creatures and snakes, refers to mythic beings, but there is no precise way to identify their meanings. The majority of Andean art works have been found in tombs, where the dry climate of Peru has preserved even fragile textiles intact for many centuries. It is not clear whether such works refer to ordinary life, like much Egyptian tomb art, or have more religious, symbolic meaning. Yet, even without perfect understanding, the marvelously sculptural ceramics and scenes on painted vases give vivid glimpses of Peruvian Indian life, as the fabrics and gold work arouse admiration for their outstanding aesthetic quality.

17.
STIRRUP-SPOUT VESSEL:
FELINE AND CACTUS PLANTS
Late Chavín, 700-500 B.C.
Peru
ceramic
h: 10 1/8 in., w: 7 3/4 in., d: 5 3/4 in.
The Nora and John Wise Collection,
gift of Mr. and Mrs. Jake L. Hamon,
the Eugene McDermott Family,
Mr. and Mrs. Algur H. Meadows
and the Meadows Foundation,
and Mr. and Mrs. John D. Murchison
1976.W62

The earliest artistically important culture in Peru is the Chavín, named after the highland site of Chavín de Huántar. The monochromatic gray-black Chavín ceramic fabric lends a powerful sculptural quality to Chavín vessels. The art of pottery was developed earlier in South America than in Middle America and seems to have spread north from there. Chavín ceramics, however, have developed far beyond the utilitarian vessels of early pot-making. They are elaborated beyond necessity and show a very inventive use of the clay medium. The stirrup-shaped handle/spout of this Chavín vessel was to have a long history in Andean art, possibly because it prevented evaporation in a dry climate. But the brilliant adapation of the feline and plant forms to the globular shape of the pot is the creative play of a master of clay modelling. Very likely the cactus plant refers to an hallucinogenic variety, while the feline may be a spirit figure: mind-enhancing drugs and animal spirits seem to have been important parts of Andean religion, as they still are among South American Indian groups today. Whatever the meaning, the tactile, sculptural quality of the vessel is very impressive.

18.
FIGURE OF A FLUTE PLAYER
Late Chavín, 700-500 B.C.
Peru, Jequetepeque Valley, Tembladera
ceramic, slips
h: 6 1/4 in., w: 3 1/2 in., d: 2 3/4 in.
Dallas Museum of Fine Arts purchase
1971.19

The remarkably sophisticated style of Chavín pottery is also apparent in the ceramic figure of a flute player. The upright figure of the man forms a solid yet elegantly ovoid, shape. To articulate this shape, raised decorative bands define his headdress, facial decorations and body costume, as though he were a ceremonial building ornamented with architectural relief. For all its small size, the figure is definitely monumental, yet it has the tactile warmth of figurative ceramics. Probably such a figure was related to ritual, for flute music has long accompanied Andean ceremonies and the flute is, besides, a very old shamanic instrument: the voice of birds and spirits. Even today flute music forms the peculiarly haunting folk music of the Andes. But who or what exactly this hieratic little image may be is unknown.

8.

19.
MANTLE (detail)
Late Paracas style (Paracas 10B), c. 450-400 B.C.
Peru: south coast, Paracas
plain weave embroidered in stem stitch; alpaca
l: 110 in., w: 51 1/2 in.
The Eugene and Margaret McDermott Fund,
in memory of John O'Boyle
1972.4.McD

A larger scale work is the impressive mantle from the south Peruvian burial site of Paracas. The Indian women who wove and embroidered this very large fabric may have worked for years on it. Presumably so lavish a creation was intended for a ruler, who may have worn it on a few occasions during his lifetime, after which it was buried with his mummy in the tomb. The mantle is both striking and subtle: its design is a checkerboard of birds and squares surrounded by an outer border of bird motifs. The main color is a rich rose-red, which is counterpointed by the soft blues, greens and yellows produced by natural dyes. Often design figures like these are incorporated into the fabric by a variety of weaving techniques; here they are embroidered. Andean textile-makers had the same inventive mastery of their medium as Andean potters.

33

19.

21.

20.
STRAP-HANDLE VESSEL: HAWK
Middle Paracas, 500-300 B.C.
Peru
ceramic, resin-suspended paint
h: 4 13/32 in., dia: 5 1/16 in.
The Nora and John Wise Collection,
gift of Mr. and Mrs. Jake L. Hamon,
the Eugene McDermott Family,
Mr. and Mrs. Algur H. Meadows
and the Meadows Foundation,
and Mr. and Mrs. John D. Murchison
1976.W85

Experimental variety is the keynote of Peruvian craftsmanship. This vessel in the Paracas style is completely
different from the Chavín pot, although it also adapts
a natural form to the shape of the vessel. The pot has
a double spout handle and is three-dimensionally
decorated in a raised pattern of bright resinous paints.
The bird form of the vessel probably represents a
falcon. The bird of prey's head is fairly naturalistic,
but the colorful raised pattern on the body is abstract
in design, recalling textile work.

21.
SPOUTED VESSEL WITH TUBULAR HANDLE:
MAN ON FISH
Gallinazo-Virú, 300-100 B.C.
Peru
ceramic
h: 7 5/16 in., w: 4 1/2 in., l: 8 5/8 in.
The Nora and John Wise Collection, Loan
W88

In a lower valley of the Peruvian north coast, the
Gallinazo-Virú style produced some inimitable vases
with whistle spouts. Due to a hole in the sphere of
the vessel, as well as other vent holes, it is possible to
produce a whistling sound by blowing down the spout.
Most of these whistling vessels are modelled with
human figures, like the charming figure of a man riding
a fish, which forms the body of this piece. Such works
may have been used as part of religious rituals, or
may simply have appealed to a native love of music,
for there is a wide variety of Andean musical instru-
ments of the woodwind kind.

22.

23.   24.

22.
SINGLE SPOUT STRAP HANDLE VESSEL: SEAL CUB
Early Nasca, 100 B.C. — A.D.200
Peru
ceramic, colored slips
h: 5 1/16 in., w: 2 7/8 in., l: 8 1/8 in.
The Nora and John Wise Collection,
gift of Mr. and Mrs. Jake L. Hamon,
the Eugene McDermott Family,
Mr. and Mrs. Algur H. Meadows
and the Meadows Foundation,
and Mr. and Mrs. John D. Murchison
1976.W154

The close observation of nature is apparent everywhere in Peruvian art. Many of the animal forms represented may be as much mythic as natural, but their expression in art reveals a keen eye, as with this pot in the form of a seal cub. It represents the Nasca style, which followed Paracas on the south coast of Peru. The seal has the combination of appealing natural charm and bold, abstract pattern so often found in Peruvian art. Nasca pottery is notable for its bright coloristic effects, now produced by clear colored slips, highly fired, which form a shiny and bright surface to the pot. The umber — tan-cream — brown range of this vessel is typical of Nasca pottery, with its russet glow.

23.
STIRRUP SPOUT VESSEL: DEER HUNTING SCENES
Moche IV, A.D.200-500
Peru
ceramic, slips
h: 10 in., w: 6 1/4 in., d: 9 1/8 in.
The Eugene and Margaret McDermott Fund
1969.2.McD

The north coast of Peru had a strongly local development through much of Peruvian history. By 200 B.C. a distinctive style had developed in the Moche and Chicama valleys of northern Peru, which, in the centuries up to 700 A.D., created a remarkably rich kind of pottery, now called Moche. In contrast with the abstract design patterns of Nasca colored pottery, Moche ceramics are often strikingly naturalistic. A whole way of life in these ancient Indian towns may be seen in Moche art.

The creative complexity of Moche pottery is evident in the pot depicting a deer hunt, which not only shows the hunt two-dimensionally in the painted scene

on the lower part of the vessel, but repeats the scene three-dimensionally on the sculptural top. This tour-de-force is executed with bold simplification, contrasting the outsize figures of hunter and deer on top with the linear narrative scene, much more naturally proportioned, circling below.

The careful depiction of contemporary dress and ornament on the figure of the hunter adds life to a genre scene, which may refer to a mythic hunt, but also is grounded in human reality.

24.
VESSEL: MAN WITH RAT AT NOSE
Moche IV, A.D.200-500
Peru
ceramic
h: 15 3/4 in., max. dia: 9 11/16 in.
The Nora and John Wise Collection,
gift of Mr. and Mrs. Jake L. Hamon,
the Eugene McDermott Family,
Mr. and Mrs. Algur H. Meadows
and the Meadows Foundation,
and Mr. and Mrs. John D. Murchison
1976.W116

This fascinating, if enigmatic, vessel is another example of the skillful Moche interplay between sculpture and flat decoration. The man's cloak, tunic and arms are painted flatly on the round body of the pot; his head, like many Moche vessels, is so lifelike as to suggest a real person. The modelled hat and the flatly painted cuff of the tunic are ornamented with similar designs, unifying the figure.

Why, though, is a rat or mouse apparently nibbling on the man's nose? This may indicate the fate of a captive or an idea from folk medicine about how to clean a wound. Or it may refer to some now lost traditional tale. Moche art certainly shows a fascination with illness and deformity, but the reference point for this scene no longer exists.

25.
PAIR OF HUMAN FIGURE EFFIGY VESSELS
Huari, A.D.600-900
Peru
ceramic, colored slips
h: 7 1/8 in., w: 4 1/16 in., d: 3 15/16 in. (left)
h: 7 9/16 in., w: 4 1/8 in., d: 4 1/16 in. (right)
The Nora and John Wise Collection,
gift of Mr. and Mrs. Jake L. Hamon,
the Eugene McDermott Family,
Mr. and Mrs. Algur H. Meadows
and the Meadows Foundation,
and Mr. and Mrs. John D. Murchison
1976.W216 and 1976.W217

After about 600 A.D. the relatively peaceful growth of local Andean societies changed. First, a major religious cult spread through Peru from the Tiahuanaco culture around Lake Titicaca in the southern Andes. Then the Huari people, from the highlands area around Ayacucho, adopted the Tiahuanaco cult and conquered large parts of Peru in a wave of aggressive militarism. Although the Huari kingdom itself had declined by 1000 A.D., the various Peruvian areas continued to be involved in warfare and in imperial ideas, such as city-building. During these years, the arts declined somewhat from the brilliantly fertile inventions of early periods, but the tradition of craftsmanship remained so strong in Peru that taste and skill never vanished.

The lesser variety found in Huari art is seen in this pair of effigy vessels, which are technically very well-made, but seem less free than Moche ceramics. The animal-monster motifs on the vases may be related to textiles, for much of the spread of the Tiahuanaco religious imagery seems to have been by way of textiles.

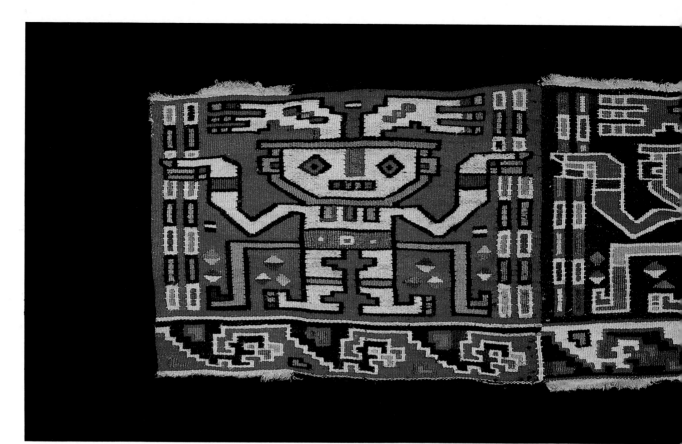

26.

27.

39

26.
BAND WITH STANDING FRONTAL FIGURES
HOLDING DOUBLE STAFFS (detail)
Moche/Huari style, c. A.D.700-800
Peru: north central coast
slit tapestry weave with occasional wefts dovetailed;
cotton warp, alpaca weft
h: 8 3/8 in.
The Eugene and Margaret McDermott Fund
1978.3.McD

A textile from the period demonstrates that, whatever
may have been the fate of pottery, textiles, which are
inherently abstract in their nature and structure, continued at a very high level. There is the repeated motif
of a figure related to the Tiahuanaco staff god, with a
step fret border above and below. The colors of the
band — carmine, cream, blue, yellow and brownish-
purple — vary in subtle ways from segment to
segment, forming a musical progression of shapes and
tones.

27.
FEATHERWORK COLLAR
Chimú style, c. A.D.1350-1476
Peru: north coast
warp-faced plain weave (cotton) with applied feathers,
beaded fringe
l: 13 1/4 in., w: 11 3/8 in.
The Eugene and Margaret McDermott Fund
1972.23.1.McD

Andean textiles were woven of cotton and alpaca wool,
but in addition the Peruvians made fabrics from the
brightly colored feathers of South American birds —
mainly macaws and parrots. These feather garments
were highly valued in their own time, being made
only for the upper class or for ritual purposes, and
today they are some of the most valuable artifacts
from Pre-Columbian Peru. This decorative collar from
the north coast of Peru is almost iridescent in its
contrasting orange and blue tones. The figurative
designs seem to be closely related to gold work made
by the people inhabiting the Lambayeque valley in
northern Peru. Cormorants, fish and human figures
appear in gold ornaments also.

28.
THREE GOLD CUPS
Lambayeque, A.D.900-1100
Peru
gold
CUP: UPSIDE-DOWN HEAD
h: 7 15/16 in., dia: 6 15/16 in. (left)
BEAKER: MAN HOLDING SCALLOP SHELL
h: 10 1/4 in., dia: 8 1/8 in. (center)
CUP: FROG MOTIF
h: 5 5/8 in., dia: 4 13/16 in. (right)
The Nora and John Wise Collection,
gift of Mr. and Mrs. Jake L. Hamon,
the Eugene McDermott Family,
Mr. and Mrs. Algur H. Meadows
and the Meadows Foundation,
and Mr. and Mrs. John D. Murchison
1976.W543, 1976.W540, 1976.W564

The Lambayeque valley was a heavily settled area and
very productive; its wealth is clear in these gold cups,
modelled in the shape of a frog and of human heads.
They are part of a find of roughly 100 gold cups from
the Lambayeque site of Batán Grande, of which 34
are in the Museum's collection. Tombs with this sort
of lavish gold work recall the awe the Spanish felt on
first seeing masses of Peruvian gold art. By 1200 A.D.
the Lambayeque area had been absorbed by the Chimú
empire and its art was merged into Chimú.

Such cups were made by the repoussé technique, in
which thin sheets of gold are hammered over a
wooden core. The cups in the shape of human heads
include ornaments like ear spools and nose decorations, which were the kind of gold adornments people actually wore. As in the Moche deer hunt vase,
with its realistic clothes and headdress, there is an
interplay between different art forms.

28.

29.

29.
TUNIC WITH GOLD SQUARES
Probably c. A.D.1471-1532
Peru: probably far south coast
warp-faced plain weave (alpaca) with appliqued gold squares
l: 34 in., w: 36 in.
The Nora and John Wise Collection,
gift of Mr. and Mrs. Jake L. Hamon,
the Eugene McDermott Family,
Mr. and Mrs. Algur H. Meadows
and the Meadows Foundation,
and Mrs. and Mrs. John D. Murchison
1976.W575

The last few centuries before the Spanish conquest
show an increasing emphasis on wealth and display,
suitable for a society committed to war and conquest.
A measure of a ruler's power was the mass of rich
grave goods left with him in the darkness of the tomb.
This shirt, from the time of the Inca Empire, is decorated with countless applied gold squares. The resulting pattern suggests a textile design transformed into
precious metal. When the Inca overran Peru in the
fifteenth century, they continued to acquire lavish art
works, especially gold and silver, as signs of their
imperial power.

41

30.
**LARGE COVER WITH MEDALLION
AND DOUBLE-HEADED BIRDS**
Colonial Period, 18th or early 19th century
Peru
interlocked tapestry weave with eccentric (non-horizontal) wefts;
cotton warp, alpaca weft
l: 75 in., w: 61 in.
Gift of the Leland Fikes Foundation, Inc.
1975.61

The conquest of Peru by the Spaniards in the 1530s
did not mean the end of all native arts. As in Mexico,
many Pre-Hispanic beliefs and practices survived
among the native people. In particular, the impressive tradition of weaving and embroidery continued,
and some ancient techniques are still in use today.
The Colonial Period tapestry textile combines Pre-
Columbian skills in weaving and dyeing with motifs
similar to the Hapsburg double eagle or the Chinese
lion from far distant civilizations. What has remained
from the past are the subtle, vibrant colors and the
centuries-old Peruvian sense of textile design.

Pre-Columbian Intermediate Area

In between the high civilizations of Peru and Middle
America, the area of Colombia, Costa Rica and Panama presented a geographical barrier of mountain and
jungle which was hard to cross in prehistoric times.
Major contacts between South America and Middle
America seem to have been by sea. The native cultures of this area were not highly developed, but the
wealth of minerals, especially alluvial gold, led to a
rich craft tradition of gold working. It is here that the
myth of El Dorado, the Golden One, first arose.

28.

30

31.
FINIAL: BIRD
Sinú, A.D.600-1200
Colombia
gold
h: 4 in., w: 2 1/2 in., l: 4 1/2 in.
The Nora and John Wise Collection,
gift of Mr. and Mrs. Jake L. Hamon,
the Eugene McDermott Family,
Mr. and Mrs. Algur H. Meadows
and the Meadows Foundation,
and Mr. and Mrs. John D. Murchison
1976.W438

32. *illustration on page 30*
PECTORAL WITH TWO HEADS IN RELIEF
Calima, A.D.400-700
Colombia
gold
h: 14 3/4 in., w: 11 1/4 in.
The Nora and John Wise Collection,
gift of Mr. and Mrs. Jake L. Hamon,
the Eugene McDermott Family,
Mr. and Mrs. Algur H. Meadows
and the Meadows Foundation,
and Mr. and Mrs. John D. Murchison
1976.W318

While there was not, in reality, a lost land built and paved with gold in this part of the Americas, tribal lords did wear lavish gold ornaments, indicating their rank and power. These precious goods were buried in their graves, where they have been rediscovered, both by archaeologists and by tomb robbers. Many of these works were made by the complex lost wax process, another example of sophisticated art made by tribal people with simple means. This delicately patterned Sinú bird finial from Colombia, a decoration which topped a chief's staff, is a piece of lost wax casting. Its design of openwork and flat circular patterns is a miracle of fine detail and elegant form.

Also from Columbia, the Calima pectoral is a repoussé work, in which sheet gold was hammered over a wooden core. It is broad and striking in effect compared with the jeweled finesse of the Sinú finial, yet also includes delicate detail in the two face masks, each of which originally had its own small nose and ear ornaments.

31.

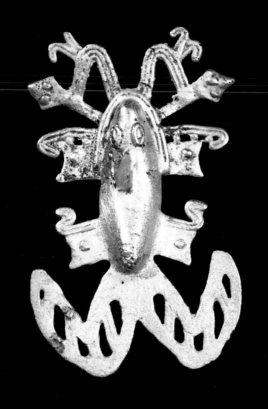

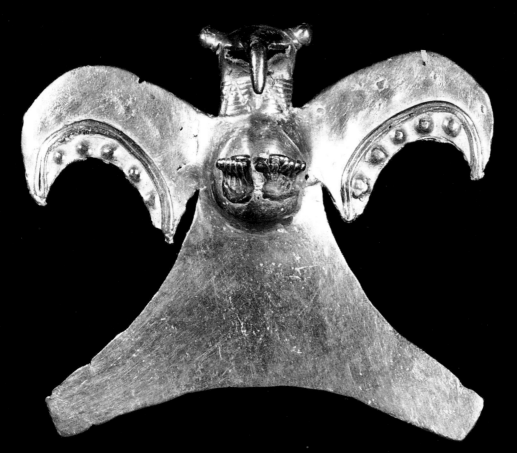

‹33.
GROUP OF PENDANTS
Veraguas, A.D.800-1200
Panama
gold
SHARK
h: 3 3/4 in., w: 2 3/8 in.
ALLIGATOR DEITY
h: 3 1/8 in., w: 2 7/8 in., d: 3/4 in.
BIRD OF PREY
h: 4 1/2 in., w: 5 3/16 in., d: 1 3/16 in.
TWO FROGS
h: 1 3/4 in., w: 2 3/16 in., d: 7/8 in.
The Nora and John Wise Collection,
gift of Mr. and Mrs. Jake L. Hamon,
the Eugene McDermott Family,
Mr. and Mrs. Algur H. Meadows
and the Meadows Foundation,
and Mr. and Mrs. John D. Murchison
1976.W303, 1976.W270, 1976.W279, 1976.W292

A group of gold ornaments from Panama indicates
the brilliant adaptation of natural forms to the demands
of jewelry. The images are flattened and bilaterally
symmetrical for maximum decorative effect. Frogs,
birds and alligators, here as in South America, probably were mythic figures.

34.
PENDANT: TWO DEITIES
Coclé, A.D.800-1200
Panama
gold
h: 3 5/16 in., w: 4 5/8 in.
The Nora and John Wise Collection,
gift of Mr. and Mrs. Jake L. Hamon,
the Eugene McDermott Family,
Mr. and Mrs. Algur H. Meadows
and the Meadows Foundation,
and Mr. and Mrs. John D. Murchison
1976.W245

The combination of myth and natural forms is even
more striking in the pendant formed by two joined
bat gods, who have both human and animal characteristics. Small as these objects are, they are conceived
with dramatic visual power. The grotesque deity figures embody the eerie feel of bats swooping in a
tropical dusk.

34.

35.

35.
BOWL
Veraguas, A.D.750-1000
Panama
polychrome ceramic
h: 2 3/4 in., dia: 9 3/16 in.
The Nora and John Wise Collection,
bequest of John Wise, 1983
1976.W51

While gold work is the best known art from this area,
admirable ceramics were also made. The dynamic circular and interlocking forms of this brightly colored
plate, with its crocodile and bird motifs, are typical
of the bravura pottery style of Veraguas.

III.

American Indian, Eskimo, and Hispanic-American Art

The Pre-Columbian civilizations grew up on a basis of native Indian craftsmanship, which may be found all over the Americas. When the Aztec conquered the Valley of Mexico in the 14th century A.D., they had only recently left their way of life as nomadic Indians in the deserts of northern Mexico. Among many Indian groups a rich tradition of religious ritual has left subtle and intricate handiworks. Some of these art traditions have survived into the present, especially among the Eskimo and the Pueblo Indians of the Southwest.

36.
MASK: BEAR SPIRIT
Eskimo
late 19th century
Alaska: Norton Sound, Yukon River Area
wood, paint, fiber, cord, feathers
h: 28 1/2 in., w: 32 5/16 in.
Gift of Mrs. Robert R. Penn
1976.49

Far north along the Arctic Circle the Eskimo practiced a shamanic religion closely related to similar cults in Siberia. Eskimo magician-shamans danced, disguised by masks, in a state of trance, through which they could communicate with a world of spirits. Masks like this one, with its wheeling feather decorations and ambivalent animal face, are ways of expressing violent emotions and controlling them through art and ritual. The ecstatic drama of the shaman's dance was a kind of psychotherapy.

37.

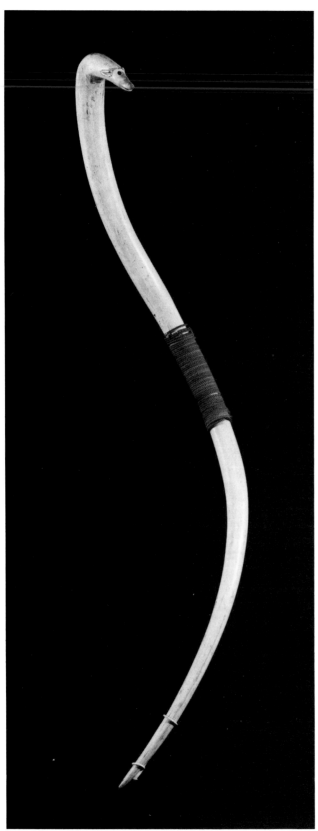

37.
MASK: SPIRIT FACE
Eskimo
late 19th century
Alaska: Lower Yukon River Area
wood, paint, gut, feathers
h: 9 13/16 in., w: 10 in.
Gift of Elizabeth Penn
1982.80

The inventive forms of Eskimo masks are matched by their psychic power. This is another example of the way the artistic skill of tribal peoples is used to embody their most profound feelings and values. The close ties between the Eskimo and nature, on which they are totally dependent in their frozen land, is expressed symbolically in the figures of waterbirds, just as their tense emotions take shape in the sinister, smiling face of the mask. The feathers, too, are both decoration and magic.

38.
SHAMAN'S STAFF
Eskimo, c. 1875
Alaska
caribou antler, baleen, fiber
h: 28 3/4 in., w: 1 in., d: 3 1/16 in.
Foundation for the Arts Collection,
gift of the Wendover Fund
and an anonymous donor
1980.1.FA

To tribal people, magic is a way of dealing with the uncontrollable elements of life, like sickness and death. The shaman is a figure of power and authority: an intermediary between human life and the Unknown. The shaman's ritual equipment was invested with the mysterious suggestiveness that found objects, such as oddly shaped stones or bones, have for the human mind. The twisted curve of this caribou antler, which was used as a shaman's staff, is made to suggest both the spirit of the animal (in the delightful animal head) and the shape of a shaman's magic bow. The extreme, pure simplicity of form is typical of Eskimo bone carving.

38.

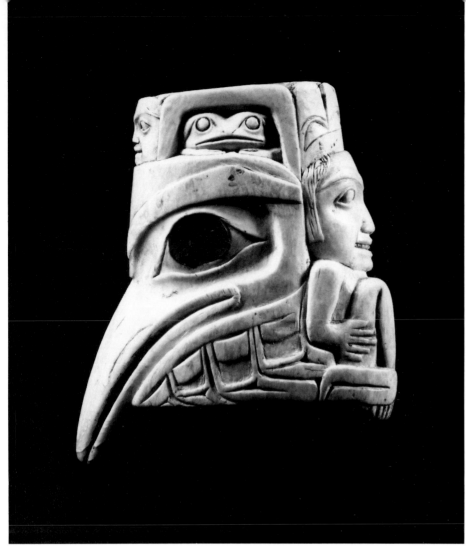

39.
LONG-BEAKED BIRD HEAD
WITH CROUCHING FIGURE AND MASKS
Haida (?), 19th century
ivory, pearl shell, wood
h: 4 1/8 in., w: 1 5/8 in., d: 3 13/16 in.
The Eugene and Margaret McDermott Fund
1977.28.McD

Almost the exact opposite in style is this ivory piece
— perhaps a knife handle — from the Northwest Coast.
Its tightly packed, allusive forms are found in much
Northwest Coast Indian carving. The main figure of a
raven is surrounded by a man's face, a frog and a
kneeling man in a feathered headdress. Such condensed imagery was like a shorthand version of mythi-
cal and heraldic tales, in which the trickster Raven
was a leading figure. This compact style was expressed
most frequently in wood carving, but could be adapted
to other media, as it is here to ivory with shell inlay.

40.
BOWL, GEOMETRIC DESIGN
Mogollon 5, Mimbres, A.D.1075-1175
United States, New Mexico
ceramic, paint
h: 6 5/16 in., w: 13 3/8 in., d: 12 in.
Gift of Martin Matyas, Bob Rheudasil,
and Mrs. Edward Marcus
in honor of Edward Marcus
1982.94

Like the Casas Grandes bowl from northern Mexico,
the Mimbres pottery of the American Southwest may
be an aftereffect of the growth of civilization in Central Mexico. Mimbres is a later phase of the Mogollon
culture, which certainly had ties with Mexico. Its clean,
hard ceramic fabric, with either black-on-white or polychrome designs, is outstanding among the great pottery styles of the prehistoric Pueblo Indians. The bowl's
vibrant, zig-zag patterns seem to capture the essence
of desert wind, lightning and storm; its forms are as
much magic symbols of nature as the Eskimo masks,
though they are pure geometry. The colors of the
bowl are natural, too: the tones of earth and desert
sand.

40.

41.

41.
CHILD'S BLANKET
Navajo, c. 1870
Arizona
wool, interlocked tapestry weave
warp: 53 1/4 in., weft: 35 1/2 in.
Foundation for the Arts Collection,
gift of Mr. and Mrs. Duncan E. Boeckman
in memory of Edward C. Reed
1978.5.FA

The Navajo herdsmen of the Southwest represented a different tradition from the settled village life of Mimbres or later Pueblo groups. A nomadic people originally, they specialized in arts like weaving, which were readily portable. On their upright looms, Navajo weavers wove blankets in subtle geometric forms related to the angular nature of weaving. The Museum's blanket is no longer purely native, as it blends synthetically dyed yarn from Europe with local hand-spun wools, but the soft changes of color across the cross, line and lozenge pattern retain a Navajo sense of design.

42.
INDIAN SOLDIER MASK,
BATTLE OF THE FIFTH OF MAY
Puebla, Zacapoaxtla, c. 1910-1930
Mexico
wood, paint, horsehair, leather, nails
h: 7 13/16 in., w: 6 1/8 in., d: 4 in.
Foundation for the Arts Collection,
gift of Mr. and Mrs. Duncan E. Boeckman
1981.81.FA

After the Spanish conquest of the New World, native Indian populations were absorbed into Spanish Catholic culture without altogether losing their individualism. In Mexico, submerged traditions often survived in the form of public dances at fiestas. While many of the masks used in these dances have European features, others, like this Indian Soldier mask from Puebla, have a stark, abstract quality recalling an older world. These layers of meaning existed in the subjects of the dances also, as the mimic battles performed by the dancers, depicting Spanish Christian wars, often treated the Spanish masters ironically, from an Indian point of view.

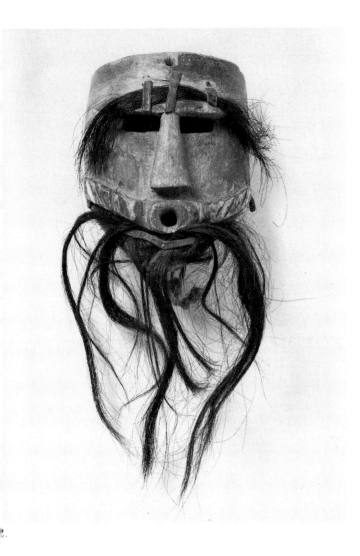

43.
SAINT FIGURES FROM NEW MEXICO:
NUESTRA SENORA DE LA LIMPIA CONCEPCIÓN
José Aragón (American, fl. 1820-1837)
wood, gesso, paint, hide, cloth
h: 25 1/2 in., w: 15 1/2 in., d: 6 7/8 in.
THE VIRGIN
José Benito Ortega (American, 1858-1941)
wood, gesso, paint, human hair, fabric, tin
h: 31 3/4 in., w: 11 1/2 in., d: 7 1/2 in.
SANTIAGO
José Benito Ortega (American, 1858-1941)
wood, gesso, paint, wool, hide, metal
h: 20 3/4 in., w: 8 1/2 in., d: 11 7/8 in.
Gifts of Mr. and Mrs. Stanley Marcus
1961.52, 1961.50, 1961.49 a-b

A more purely Spanish adaptation to life in the New
World is the creation of Christian *santo* figures in
New Mexico. From the mid-18th century on these
wooden carvings of Jesus, Mary and popular Catholic
saints were made by humble Spanish - American artisans, living on the farthest edge of the Spanish Empire,
yet still trying to express deep religious feelings of
the Catholic faith in their handiwork. The grace, dignity and immediate charm of these works testify to
the artist's success.

43.

53.

IV.

African Art

The kingdoms and farming villages of Black Africa stretched over much of the continent in a great central band running from the Atlantic Ocean, south of the Sahara desert, through grassland and tropical forest, to the mountains, plains and coast of the Indian Ocean in East Africa. While the peoples in this giant territory differed much in language and history, they shared a tribal way of life and they created art styles intimately related to their religion.

In most of the traditional African societies there were few characterized gods; instead, there was an all-pervading awareness of ancestors, who were believed not to have died forever, but to live on in spirit form, influencing their descendents. Magic, witchcraft, curing and ceremonial dances all involved efforts to communicate with this great supernatural force and power. African sculptures achieved a powerful form because they were thought to be impregnated with magic efficacy. Often substances like powder, blood, palm oil or camwood paste were rubbed onto the sculpture to increase its potency.

African art deals with primary things — birth, initiation, fertility, death — seen as part of a web of past and present. It is about generation in both senses of the word: the ancestors of the tribe and human sexuality, which passes on life to the future. The abstract shapes of African art, so admired by 20th-century artists, are due to its archetypal character.

44.

45.
RHYTHM POUNDER *(Déblé)*
Senufo (Siena)
Ivory Coast: Northern Region, Sikasso District
wood, red abrus seeds, cowry shells
h: 36 3/8 in., w: 8 1/4 in., d: 6 in.
The Gustave and Franyo Schindler Collection of African Sculpture,
gift of the McDermott Foundation in honor of Eugene McDermott
1974.Sc15

While the aesthetic effect of African sculpture is intense, this creative vitality comes not only from the individual gifts of the carver (conscious though he may be of his skills), but also from the shared values of his village group and the ritual importance of the work. Here again is a standing female figure, this time forming a rhythm pounder, which was used in the rituals of age-grade societies among the Senufo.

The oval curves of the figure suggest the slow, repeated rhythm with which the pounder struck the earth. Again, the face is mask-like, and scarcely feminine at all, in the terms of Western art. The woman's sexual parts are purely symbolic; they form part of the whole figure's elegant, yet massive, design. Energy flows up and down the curving forms, paralleling the initiate's movements as he moves the beater up and down.

44.
STANDING FEMALE FIGURE
late 19th century
Master of Ogol
Dogon
Mali
wood, patination, metal, beads
h: 22 7/8 in., w: 4 1/2 in., d: 5 9/16 in.
The Gustave and Franyo Schindler Collection of African Sculpture,
gift of the McDermott Foundation in honor of Eugene McDermott
1974.Sc5

African sculpture may be seen as a series of variations on the human figure. Since wood sculptures were carved from whole sections of tree trunks, they tend to retain the columnar feel of the tree. As they were shaped by the metal edges of knife and adze, the forms are boldly outlined, in sweeping cuts and lines. These are the technical means of African sculpture; the brilliant simplifications of form seen in this female figure from the Dogon people of Mali owe as much to the traditional idea of a cult image, as to technique alone. This is *woman:* a powerful symbol, with jutting conical breasts and mask-like head. As in most African sculptures, the head, center of intelligence and life, dominates and the torso is elongated. The legs are flexed, as in ritual dance. Every part of the figure is filled with up-springing muscular energy.

45.

46.

46.
EQUESTRIAN FIGURE
Senufo (Siena), Central Region
Ivory Coast
wood, patination
h: 12 5/8 in., w: 2 7/8 in., d: 8 3/4 in.
The Gustave and Franyo Schindler Collection of African Sculpture,
gift of the McDermott Foundation in honor of Eugene McDermott
1974.Sc14

As is true in most tribal societies, magicians or witch doctors were believed to communicate with a supernatural world. Since Africans thought the dead did not really "die", but remained an influence on the present, it was readily thought that spirit familiars could pass back and forth between living and dead. Both witches and curers drew their power from this spirit realm. This figure of a horseman is a messenger, or intermediary, between Man and the Otherworld. In its geometric clarity one can almost see the carver's knife slashing the horizontal planes of this figure, but it is not abstraction for its own sake: it is a spirit horseman on a ghostly horse.

47.
NIMBA HEADDRESS
Baga
Guinea
wood
h: 48 1/2 in., w: 16 1/8 in., d: 27 11/16 in.
The Gustave and Franyo Schindler Collection of African Sculpture,
gift of the McDermott Foundation in honor of Eugene McDermott
1974.Sc18

The presence of a supernatural being is overpoweringly expressed in the fertility goddess represented by this massive headdress from the Baga tribe. While the seventy-five pound figure is only part of the whole costume worn by a ritual dancer, whose raffia garment concealed completely his human appearance, the headdress alone has a commanding presence. The jutting, bird-like forms of the head and breasts create awe, while promising bountiful crops in the future. In the farming rites of the Baga, the dancer, weighed down and disguised by this headdress, was transformed into a spirit being himself. The symbolic presentation of divinity occurs in both art and ritual. Even the worn-out, rotting *nimba* was treated with great reverence, for magic still clung to it.

48.

47.

48.
HEAD EFFIGY BELL
Lower Niger, Forcados River Style
Nigeria
bronze
h: 5 5/8 in., dia: 2 7/8 in.
Gift of Margaret and Eugene McDermott
1976.3

Moving eastward from West Africa, one finds the exuberant art of Nigeria, still a center of African creativity today. Although the bulk of African art is wood sculpture (which decays rapidly in a tropical climate), Africans are highly accomplished metalworkers, too. The bronze sculptures of Benin are famous examples. This is an ancient bronze bell from the lower Niger River region, cast by the lost wax process. Its raised ornamental surfaces add a somber decorative richness to the effigy head, while the horns and snake figures indicate its magic power.

49.
TAPPER FOR IFA DIVINATION (*Iro Ifa*)
Yoruba
Nigeria
ivory
h: 7 7/8 in., w: 1 1/2 in., d: 2 in.
Museum League Travel Fund
1978.40

Divination to detect the will of spirits and the causes of misfortune is practiced everywhere in Africa, usually with a divining object, which may be manipulated while the diviner is consulting the oracles. This Yoruba piece, elegantly shaped to fit the diviner's hand, is probably a female devotee of Ifa, the demigod of divination, who brought knowledge and help to mankind.

49.

‹50.
DANCE HEADDRESS
Ibo
Nigeria
wood, paint, metal, fiber
h: 18 1/2 in., w: 12 7/8 in., d: 10 7/8 in.
The Eugene and Margaret McDermott Fund
1975.27.McD

The suave, small-scale Ifa tapper may be contrasted
with the almost coarse vitality of this Ibo headdress,
which also involves supernatural communication. Jagged,
aggressive, and roughly hewn, it is an image of the
powers of witchcraft. The birds projecting from this
complex structure are the familiars of witches and
ghosts. Like the *nimba* headdress, to wear this massive object was to assume a spirit role.

51.
STANDING FEMALE FIGURE
Ibo
Nigeria
wood, paint, metal, fiber, glass beads
h: 36 7/8 in., w: 8 3/4 in., d: 8 1/2 in.
The Gustave and Franyo Schindler Collection of African Sculpture,
gift of the McDermott Foundation in honor of Eugene McDermott
1974.Sc29

A similar tough power may be seen in the female
shrine figure from Nigeria. The elaborate, crested hairdo
refers to actual hairdos, which conveyed a woman's
rank and family. Here the curving forms add to the
monumental, non-human strength of the sculpture. It
is full of raw power: the figure seems ready to leap
into the air, yet is solidly grounded on the earth stamped
by the woman's heavy feet. It is in a state of almost
unbearable balance: poised, tense, weighty, a coiled
spring of dense energy. These are the vital powers of
people from whom clan and family life descend.

51.

52.

52.
RELIQUARY GUARDIAN FIGURE
Sogo
Gabon
wood, kaolin, black paint, metal
h: 20 3/8 in., w: 8 1/8 in., d: 5 3/4 in.
The Gustave and Franyo Schindler Collection of African Sculpture,
gift of the McDermott Foundation in honor of Eugene McDermott
1974.Sc37

The extraordinary ability to express physical weight and energy in African art is apparent in this reliquary guardian figure from Gabon, which, even more than the Ibo female figure, has the stark simplicity of a timeless image. Such figures were set up over the containers which held the bones of the dead, to act as guardians. In this sculpture the bare irreducible minimum of humanity can be seen, but it is far from impassive: the mouth speaks; the jutting ears and arms command attention. It is hieratic with the simplest of means. Masters of positive and negative space, African carvers made each part of an image echo the others. Traces of charcoal and white pigment add to the effect.

53. *illustration on page 52*
SEATED FEMALE FIGURE WITH CHILD
Yombe
Zaire
wood, glass or mica
h: 15 in.
The Clark and Frances Stillman Collection of Congo Sculpture,
gift of Eugene and Margaret McDermott
1969.S21

A considerable part of the Museum's display of African art is part of the Clark and Frances Stillman Collection, which covers the art of Zaire (the old Belgian Congo). In the Stillman pieces it is possible to see an even more concentrated series of variations in figurative sculpture, mostly small-to-medium scale, than in the works from West Africa. The essentially symbolic character of African art is evident in the Yombe mother and child group which is wholly without the human tenderness one would find in a Madonna from the European tradition. This is Motherhood, a principle of life. The baby is a toy or fetish in the lap of a majestic spirit woman, whose body is taut with energy. Bits of glass and mica give the face an hypnotic glitter, adding to the impression that it is a magic object.

54.
STANDING FIGURE
Boma
Zaire
wood
h: 11 3/4 in.
The Clark and Frances Stillman Collection of Congo Sculpture,
gift of Eugene and Margaret McDermott
1969.S6

The subtle kinds of geometric reduction of the human form possible in this kind of ritual art appear in the Boma Standing Figure. There is none of the descriptive richness found in the Yombe woman; the sculpture is a pattern of diamond shapes. Yet the force of both works depends on their magical purpose.

54.

55.

56.

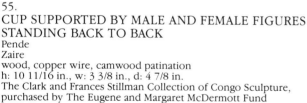

55.
CUP SUPPORTED BY MALE AND FEMALE FIGURES
STANDING BACK TO BACK
Pende
Zaire
wood, copper wire, camwood patination
h: 10 11/16 in., w: 3 3/8 in., d: 4 7/8 in.
The Clark and Frances Stillman Collection of Congo Sculpture,
purchased by The Eugene and Margaret McDermott Fund
1978.51.McD

Another strongly geometric work is the Pende cup,
perhaps a marriage cup. Two figures, male and female,
form mirror images of each other and support the
finely decorated vessel. The balance of man and woman,
which supports African society and carries on the
family, is a common theme in African art. The loving
care with which the carver approached such a piece
is seen in the movement from the flat, relatively broad
and crude feet, which support the figures, to the minute hatching of the hair and sides of the cup.

56.
STANDING MALE FIGURE
Chokwe
Zaire/Angola
wood, metal, leather
h: 14 1/2 in.
The Clark and Frances Stillman Collection of Congo Sculpture,
gift of Eugene and Margaret McDermott
1969.S1

A much more massive effect is achieved by the Chokwe
standing male figure. There is no decoration: the smooth,
solid forms are ornamented only by projections like
the hair, bracelets and penis.

58.⟩

57.
STANDING FEMALE FIGURE
Luba
Zaire
wood, beads, skin
h: 13 in.
The Clark and Frances Stillman Collection of Congo Sculpture,
gift of Eugene and Margaret McDermott
1969.S96

By contrast, this Luba standing female figure is all
delicacy and decoration. The body is so thin it seems
like a straight line and is covered with a jewel-like
pattern of textures formed by the woman's sexual
parts, scarification patterns, neck beads and hairdo.
Both the raised scar patterns and the intricately braided
hair arrangements of African women indicate their
family and status. Sometimes, as here, they become
part of the design of a sculpture; sometimes they are
simplified or ignored. The woman clasps her breasts
in an age-old gesture of fertility.

58.
STOOL SUPPORTED BY KNEELING
FEMALE FIGURE
Luba
Zaire
wood, beads, metal
h: 16 in.
The Clark and Frances Stillman Collection of Congo Sculpture,
gift of Eugene and Margaret McDermott
1969.S105

The ingenuity with which a shape may be adapted to
a function is clear in this chief's stool. The woman, a
true Earth Mother, supports the seat, as the tribe supports its ruler. Her head is immense and handsome;
her torso is squat; her legs are mere circles of support.
She could be a village woman carrying a tray or basket on her head; naturalism and abstraction blend
perfectly. Scar patterns, beads and hair style form a
restrained decoration for the stool. The lavish carving
of the piece indicates that it was not simply something to sit on, but a symbol of authority.

59.
HEADREST SUPPORTED BY A STANDING
FEMALE FIGURE
Lulua
Zaire
wood
h: 7 in., w: 4 1/4 in., d: 3 7/16in.
The Clark and Frances Stillman Collection of Congo Sculpture,
purchased by the Eugene and Margaret McDermott Fund
1978.48.McD

The elaborate hair arrangements of African women take many hours to oil and braid. To protect these almost heraldic creations at night, people slept on headrests, which supported their coiffures. The Lulua headrest has a carved support in the form of a woman with an extensive overall pattern of waffle scarification.

59.

60.

60.
STANDING FEMALE FIGURE
Lulua
Zaire
wood, patination
h: 26 27/32 in., w: 4 in., d: 3 7/16in.
The Clark and Frances Stillman Collection of Congo Sculpture,
purchased by the Eugene and Margaret McDermott Fund
1978.49.McD

Scarification was a painful initiation process under-
gone by young men and women as a test for adult
life. Clay rubbed into cuts left a permanent raised
scar on the body. Whether people actually had this
amount of scar patterns is debatable, but Lulua sculpture emphasizes the conversion of the human body
into art. The scarification of this figure forms a kind
of second, ornamental skin on the columnar body.

61.
STANDING MALE FIGURE
Songe
Zaire
wood, horn, skin, fiber
h: 18 1/2 in.
The Clark and Frances Stillman Collection of Congo Sculpture,
gift of Eugene and Margaret McDermott
1969.S173

Magic and Power are the essence of African art, of
which its remarkable formal invention is only the outer
skin. The pulsing force, at once sensual and remote,
which gives African sculptures their vitality, springs
from ritual. The Songe standing male figure is unquali-
fied magic: it has a horn on its head, to bring protection,
and the snakeskin attached to it serves the same purpose. In its small form, ponderous with the weight of
the past, it crystallizes the power of ancestors and
spirits. It is a fetish or protective amulet.

61.

62.

62.
HELMET MASK
Tetela
Zaire
wood, paint
h: 23 3/4 in., w: 13 1/2 in., d: 11 1/2 in.
The Clark and Frances Stillman Collection of Congo Sculpture,
purchased by the Eugene and Margaret McDermott Fund
1971.12.McD

The power concentrated inwardly in ancestor statues
or fetishes is projected outward in the masks of African ceremonials. Both masks and statues express deep
human feelings and bring hidden terrors, like illness
or death, out into the open, where they may be
exorcised. The non-human, awe-inspiring character
of African masks is a disguise, through which people
may dramatize conflicts and transcend them. All forms
of African art have this ability to visualize another
realm of existence and to transport people, as did the
Senufo horseman, to a spirit realm.

V.

Indonesian Art

Art styles similar in nature and function to African art may be found among the native peoples of the Indonesian archipelago. These groups' way of life may go back as far as Neolithic times, and has remained, even in the 20th century, largely untouched by the influence of Hinduism, Buddhism or Islam, which had such a powerful effect on the rest of Indonesia. In Sumatra, in Sulawesi, in the small islands between Java and New Guinea, many village people retained their archaic cults and ancestral spirits, as well as practices like head-hunting, which form a very old stratum in this part of the Orient. Their figural arts were devoted primarily to wood carvings, which often expressed their devotion to semi-divine clan founders.

63.
ARCHITECTURAL ORNAMENT *(Singa)*
Batak (Lake Toba Region)
Indonesia: Sumatra
wood
h: 51 in., w: 21 1/2 in., d: 18 1/2 in.
Gift of J. Gabriel Barbier-Müller
1980.22

The highly expressive architectural wood carvings of the Batak people may be seen in their decorative building ornaments. This figure is called *singa,* or lion, though it actually is an imaginary monster, locally believed to bring fertility and prosperity. Such *singa* images were placed in prominent positions over houses, as magic charms. The intricate overall decoration on the figure only highlights the hypnotic effect of the staring eyes.

63.

⟨65.

64.

64.
FUNERARY FIGURE *(tau tau)*
Indonesia: Sulawesi (Celebes)
wood
h: 32 11/16 in., w: 9 3/8 in., d: 6 3/4 in.
The Eugene and Margaret McDermott Fund
1980.2.McD

The importance of ancestor figures is evident in this funerary image from Sulawesi (the Celebes). The Toradja made elaborate effigies to accompany the body of a dead person; these effigies were fully clothed and were left in rock-cut cave shrines. The figures are called *tau-tau* or ''little person''. They were fed and given offerings long after the funeral ceremonies for which they were carved. The Museum's *tau-tau* figure, dating to the late 19th century, is a gripping image with a haunted, intense expression.

65. *illustration on page 68*
ANCESTOR FIGURE
Indonesia: Ataoro
wood, fiber, cloth
h: 19 15/16 in., w: 3 15/16 in., d: 4 3/4 in.
Museum League Purchase Fund
1981.15

From the small group of Ataoro villages in the Lesser
Sunda Islands comes this very rare ancestral figure,
originally designed to be set in a shrine dedicated to
the founders of a clan. It is formally perfect: a series
of pure, curving lines which complement each other
harmoniously. Like African ancestor figures, its severely
reduced forms suggest mythic power, while the added
textures of twine and cloth add life to the solid wooden
figure.

66.
SHRINE FIGURE: FEMALE ANCESTOR
Indonesia: Ataoro
wood
h: 27 5/32 in., w: 3 1/32 in., d: 3 7/8 in.
Gift of Helen Bankston, Sally Brice, Ginny Eulich,
Margaret Folsom, Mary Ellen Fox, Betty Jo Hay,
La Verne McCall, Judy Tycher,
and an anonymous donor
1983.49

Ataoro ancestor figures were usually mounted in pairs,
one male and one female. The Museum is fortunate to
have an example of a female figure, also. It is quite
different in style from the male figure, being tall and
thin, and so flat as to seem rather disembodied. Two
stylized children are carved on the front of the body,
which is otherwise ornamented only by a delicate
pendant and two tiny breasts. It is a pillar-like monument to the world of gods, from which human beings
descend.

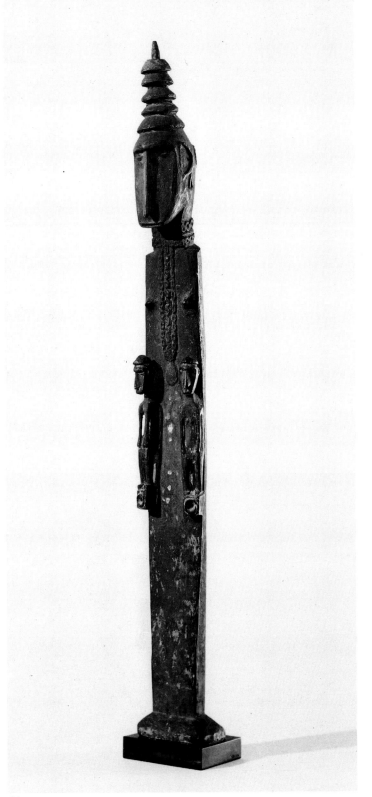

66.

67.

VI.

Oceanic Art

Farther east, the tribal peoples of New Guinea and the islands of Melanesia also produced art comparable to Africa or indigenous Indonesia. Masks and figure sculptures were designed for religious ceremonies, while objects of everyday use, such as house posts, canoe prows or food containers, were decorated with symbolic designs. However, in comparison with African or Indonesian art, Oceanic carvings are remarkable for a wide range of applied materials, including shells, feathers, vegetable fibers, shark's teeth and barkcloth, as well as European fabrics and dyes, all of which created rich textures and fantastic outlines.

67.
ULI FIGURE
Melanesia: New Ireland, Central Region
wood, paint, chalk, opercula, pearl shell,
plant fibers, resinous paint
h: 53 5/8 in., w: 18 7/16 in.
The Roberta Coke Camp Fund
1975.14

Another striking characteristic of Oceanic art is the degree to which it may dramatize psychological states of aggression and fear. It can be startlingly violent in its emotional impact, unlike the controlled balance one usually sees in African sculpture. This may be due to the emphasis on warfare and competition in Oceanic societies. The ancestral *Uli* figure from New Ireland has a fiercely combative expression and an overtly bi-sexual character which is equally fierce. This is no benign clan ancestor, but rather a threatening figure, whose sexuality is allied to magic and violence.

68.
MALE ANCESTOR FIGURE NAMED *MALABI*
Sawos Group
Melanesia: New Guinea, Middle Sepik River Region,
Yamok Village,
Dambwibit Cult House of Wolembi Sector
wood, fiber, lime, traces of paint
h: 89 1/2 in., w: 13 1/4 in., d: 9 in.
The Eugene and Margaret McDermott Fund
1974.5.McD

Another example of the ties between art and the cult of the dead may be seen in the large ancestor figure from the Sawos tribe in New Guinea. Although the figure represents an actual person, the elongated, staring sculpture appears to be an archetype. It may also have been a skull rack; head-hunting and ritual cannibalism were common in New Guinea societies. Its splendidly stylized and ornamental forms show that it is possible to make beauty out of terror: this visitant from dreams or the unconscious mind is depicted in a great formal composition, dominated by the large oval head, with its haunting eyes. Elements of the man's anatomy, like his eyes, nose, breasts, navel, and kneecaps, appear as jeweled tracery on the abstract shape of the body.

70.

68.

69.

69.
MASK
19th century
Melanesia: New Ireland, Northwestern Region, Nusa(?)
wood, paint, obsidian chips, cane, plant fibers,
bark cloth, shagged bark
h: 13 1/8 in., w: 24 1/2 in., d: 14 3/4 in.
The Roberta Coke Camp Fund
1975.12

Quite possibly, the very frequency of war and violence in Melanesian life, which led to the expression
of ambiguous terrors in their art, may explain the
evocative psychic power of masks like this one. The
brutal force of the image, with its piercing eyes and
shark-like mouth, is lightened and enriched by the
marvelous counterpoint of textures — barkcloth, palm
fiber, obsidian chip eyes — and the colorful overall
painted pattern of the face. There is a strong feeling
of fantasy and imaginative release in this vision of a
tough supernatural being.

70.
STILT STEP
19th century
Polynesia: Marquesas Islands
wood
h: 15 5/8 in., w: 2 3/4 in., d: 4 in.
Foundation for the Arts Collection,
gift of the Alvin and Lucy Owsley Foundation
1976.4.FA

The Polynesians, who settled the islands of the central Pacific, had a more peaceful way of life and a
smoother, more suave, art style than the Melanesians.
The carved foot support for ceremonial stilts, made
in the Marquesas Islands, is a good example of the
Polynesian gift for overall decoration. The larger and
smaller heads echo each other as accents on the triangu-
lar forms. The rounded, smooth solidity of the figure
is far removed from the bravura tensions of the
Melanesian pieces.

71.

VII.

Oriental Art

There are a number of parallels between the arts of eastern Asia and the Pre-Columbian arts of the New World. In both areas highly skilled craftsmen, working in stone, wood, jade, clay and textiles, produced intricate works either for temples or for the aristocracy. These arts were closely tied to religion, as they illustrated myths or ornamented sacred buildings. Secular works were related in style to religious works. Meaning and technique were intertwined.

India

In India most art was created for the two great religions which developed there, Hinduism and Buddhism. Kingdoms might rise and fall, invasions might alter significantly the course of Indic history, great cities or shrines might be abandoned to decay, but the impulse to build and create for the gods scarcely wavered. Today, the great temple complexes of medieval India still stand as monuments to a religious vision at once sensuous and mystical.

The basic nature of Hinduism goes back to the Aryan invasions of India around 1500 B.C., when an Indo-European speaking people imposed their way of life on the native inhabitants of the Indian peninsula. The Aryan gods were closely related to the original deities of the Greeks, Celts and Germans, but the meeting between Aryan and non-Aryan led to a peculiarly Indic emphasis on caste, asceticism and ritual purity. Later forms of Hinduism included a vast panorama of gods and myths.

Buddhism began as a reaction against this proliferating wealth of myth and the accompanying Hindu commitment to self-mortifying austerity. Siddhartha, the historical founder of Buddhism, achieved Enlightenment, not by yogic penances but by perceiving the Middle Way, a moderate, humanist self-discipline which detached the soul from ignorance and desire. For more than a thousand years after the Buddha's lifetime in the 6th century B.C., Buddhism had great success in India, and also spread to Sri Lanka, Southeast Asia, Tibet, China and Japan. Eventually it almost disappeared in India itself.

71. *illustration on page 76*
BUST OF A BODHISATTVA
Indian, Kushan Period,
Gandharan Style, A.D. 2nd-3rd century
Pakistan: Peshawar Region
gray schist
h: 28 3/8 in., w: 20 in.
Gift of Mr. and Mrs George V. Charlton
1973.81

The Buddhist arts of India were to have great influence outside their native land. The iconography of Buddhism was carried along the trade routes to China and by merchant ships to Southeast Asia. One of the most important early types of Buddhist art was the figure of the Bodhisattva, a person who had achieved Enlightenment but had voluntarily chosen to return to the world to help mankind. This messiah-like image combined humanity with divinity, whereas images of the Buddha were intended to be purely divine and dematerialized.

India was always most vulnerable to land invasions along the northwest frontier in Afghanistan. It was from here that Alexander the Great made his brief foray into northern India. Also from here Greek, and later Roman, art was to have a marked influence on Indic art, especially in the Gandharan style. Buddhist images like this Bodhisattva recall the athlete figures and drapery of the Mediterranean world. Even the Bodhisattva's sacred topknot, symbolizing enlightenment, may be an echo of Greco-Roman art.

However, in a work like this, the forms of classical art have been thoroughly converted to Indic taste. The benign Buddhist figure is represented as a handsome prince, draped in lavish, jeweled ornaments. He is sumptuous and fleshy, yet tender, as he raises his right hand in the gesture of benevolence. Such clean, crisp forms and strong sensual impact may be found in Hindu as well as Buddhist sculptures.

72.
VISHNU WITH ATTENDANTS
Solanki Period, c. A.D.1026
India: Gujarat
sandstone
h: 53 in., w: 26 1/2 in., d: 10 1/2 in.
Gift of Mrs John Leddy Jones
1963.29

Just as a Buddhist sacred figure could be represented as an Indic prince, so the gods of Hinduism were frequently shown in regal costume. By the 11th century A.D. Buddhism had almost disappeared in India and Hinduism was divided between the rival cults of the great gods Vishnu (the Preserver) and Shiva (the Destroyer). An architectural relief in sandstone represents Vishnu surrounded by his court of heavenly attendants. Most Hindu temples were themselves a kind of large-scale sculpture, as they were covered with a labyrinth of carved images like this one.

Vishnu is depicted in flat frontal relief, dominating the plane of lower relief figures behind him. The effect of the whole is an intricate pattern of shapes, and this is even more striking when such a work is *in situ* on a temple wall, with strong contrasts of sun and shade. The image of Vishnu appears as an ideal Hindu prince with a slim body and elegant ornaments. He is also God: he holds in his four hands, symbolic of supernatural power, the mace, conch shell, discus and jewels of divine wisdom.

73.

73.
DOOR JAMB RELIEF: DIKAPALA (?) AND ATTENDANTS
Chandella Dynasty, A.D. 11th century
India: Rajasthan
sandstone
h: 22 5/16 in., w: 12 3/8 in., d: 6 7/8 in.
Gift of Sarah Dorsey Hudson
1982.30

A similar architectural piece is this 11th century A.D. door jamb from the Chandella Dynasty in Rajasthan, which represents a directional god with attendant figures. The relief is both more three-dimensional and more erotic than the Vishnu relief. The almost nude female figures, based on Indian temple dancers, have a twining richness of form, and even the central figure has a voluptuous stance. The plastic architectural forms are equally physical. One of the most impressive features of Indic temple decoration is this ability to weave figures and background into a sensuous whole with multiple angles and deeply cut textures.

74.
DANCER
A.D. 10th-12th century
India: Rajasthan, Mount Abu
marble
h: 42 1/2 in., w: 14 in., d: 9 1/2 in.
Gift of the Alvin and Lucy Owsley Foundation
1973.98

The Museum's marble figure of a dancer fully conveys religious eroticism. The pose is based on actual positions of classic temple dance, but the woman is an archetype, full-breasted, narrow waisted and ideally beautiful. She embodies the Hindu belief that all sensuous experiences are a revelation of divinity. The sharply undercut forms make the sculpture open to the caressing play of light in the same way as the Chandella relief.

74.

75.

75.
DANCING DAKINI VAJRAVARAHI
c. A.D. 1600
Tibet
gilt bronze with inlaid semi-precious stones
h: 9 7/8 in., w: 5 3/4 in., d: 2 3/4 in.
Foundation for the Arts Collection,
purchased with a grant from
the Virginia C. and Floyd C. Ramsey Fund
of Communities Foundation
of Texas, Incorporated
1982.9.FA

Although Buddhism declined in medieval India, it remained a major religion elsewhere in eastern Asia. In Tibet Buddhism took the form of Tantric cults, magical and erotic religious rites heavily influenced by Hinduism. A Buddhist goddess figure from Tibet shows obvious ties with Indic dance images and may be related to Hindu forms of the Mother Goddess, Varahi. Both the sensuous character of the image and the violent death imagery found in the goddess' fanged mouth, string of skulls, cup of blood and executioner's axe, recall the identification of sexuality and death associated with Hindu goddesses like Kali.

This is a rich and dynamic work. The contrast between the jeweled luxury of the inlaid gilt-bronze sculpture and the grim underlying meaning occurs frequently in Tantric art, where sex and death are seen as part of one universal reality, to be expressed in art by glowing colors, exuberant rhythms, lavish ornament and expressive, earthy vigor.

China

A majority of the Museum's Chinese works are ceramics. The art of fine pottery manufacture was highly admired in ancient China; one mark of a distinguished connoisseur was his knowledge of ceramic styles. Unlike pottery from the New World, which was hand-formed by a single potter, Chinese vessels were often the work of numerous skilled artisans employed by a ceramic workshop. Several people might work on a single piece. From at least the second millenium B.C., pottery was thrown on the potter's wheel and was kiln-fired. These conditions led to experiments with the glazes used to decorate the surfaces of the vessels and to the development of new ornamental ideas. The extraordinary variety and technical brilliance of Chinese ceramics indicate why porcelain is still called "china" in English.

76.

76.
JAR WITH IMPRESSED DESIGN
Late Zhou Dynasty, 600-256 B.C.
China
ceramic
h: 11 9/16 in., dia: 13 3/4 in.
The Art Museum League Fund
1973.79

The first stages of most pottery traditions are earthenwares, which are relatively soft-bodied fabrics fired at low temperatures. This extremely satisfying jar from the late Zhou dynasty has a dark earthenware body covered with a gray glaze formed by ash during the firing of the vessel. It was these early natural glazes which led to the development of colored ash glazes in later periods.

The solid, ample form of the jar reflects the long-lasting Chinese desire for stability and harmony in pottery design. The overall impressed pattern, made by a wooden stamp, is an effective counterpart to the rotund simplicity of the vessel's shape.

77.

77.
LONGQUAN TIGER VASE WITH SWAN COVER
Song Dynasty, 12th century A.D.
China
porcelain, celadon glaze
h: 10 5/8 in. (with cover), w: 5 in.
Munger Fund purchase
1971.16.a and b

Centuries of experimentation with both the fabric and the glazes of pottery led to the creation of true porcelain. Porcelains are made from kaolin, a very fine white clay found in only a few sites in China. This clay body is covered by a vitreous glaze composed largely of feldspar. When fired at high temperatures porcelain has a hard clear body and a translucent, reflective surface.

One of the most treasured kinds of porcelain glaze was celadon, a gray-green glaze resembling jade. Also, celadons often have a subtle crackled surface beneath the glaze. A high point in celadon manufacture was the wares produced during the Song dynasty, which, in general, was a great period for Chinese ceramics. The Museum is fortunate to have a complete Song Longquan vase with its original lid.

All parts of this elegant vessel are formed into a sculptural whole which is unified by the celadon green sheen. The body of the vase is incised with a lotus pattern, while a small tiger curves around the neck of the vessel. On the lid is a swan. The two animals seem charming and natural outgrowths of the vase's curving forms.

78.
TEA BOWL WITH PERSIMMON DESIGN
Song Dynasty, A.D. 13th century
China
ceramic, *temmoku* glaze, iron oxide decoration
h: 3 in., dia: 7 5/8 in.
Gift of Mrs Alex Camp
in memory of Mrs A.C. Bigger
1971.15

Another example of the refined delicacy of Song style is the tea bowl covered in *temmoku* glaze. These dark glazes, through which underglaze patterns appear to shimmer mysteriously, are a perfect reflection of the Song taste for ambiguous, poetically evocative art. Such cups were used in tea ceremonies and have a deliberately casual appearance, which belies the fact they are actually works of considerable technical complexity. Art conceals art. The persimmon figures of the underglaze design are hardly recognizable as natural forms; they seem to be ephemeral drops of glaze floating in the dark pool of the cup.

78.

79.

Japan

79.
JAR WITH MOLDED AND IMPRESSED DESIGN
Middle Jōmon Period, 3000-2500 B.C.
Japan
terra cotta
h: 17 1/2 in., w: 12 in.
Foundation for the Arts Collection,
gift of The Wendover Fund
1965.15.FA

To go from the elegant Chinese tea bowl to the early
Japanese Jōmon jar is to enter another visual world.
The ample calm admired by the Chinese is replaced
by a boldly asymmetrical and dramatic creation, whose
flaring shapes almost deny the nature of pottery. This
bravura tension was to recur often in Japanese art.
Like the Chinese Zhou jar, the Jōmon jar is a piece of
earthenware decorated by impressed designs, but there
is no other point of contact. The Japanese potter has
twisted clay into fantastic curves, and the cord-impressed
patterns also weave and flow in ornamental lines. The
vessel is alive with nervous vitality.

80.

80.
AMIDA NYORAI
(BUDDHA OF THE WESTERN PARADISE)
Late Fujiwara or early Kamakura Period,
c. A.D.1175-1200
Japan
gilded lacquer on wood
h: 34 1/2 in., w: 11 1/2 in. (base), d: 10 1/2 in.
The Art Museum League Fund
1978.26

Buddhism was introduced from China into Japan in the 6th century A.D. The new religion, as well as an increased acquaintance with Chinese writing and art, had an important influence on Japanese civilization, although Japanese art continued to have a distinctive character. The subjects of Buddhist art were readily adopted by the Japanese. At first Buddhism was chiefly a religion patronized by the aristocracy, but in the troubled years which followed the decline of Fujiwara rule in the 12th century A.D., a more accessible kind of Buddhism became widespread and popular. This Pure Land school of religion promised salvation to everyone who called on Buddha's name.

The gilt wooden statue of Amida, the Buddha of Light who welcomed souls to the Western Paradise, or Pure Land, reflects the gentle, consoling character of popular Buddhism. The delicate small-featured figure, depicted with the quiet grace of late Fujiwara style, presents the promise of peace. Yet the work is unmistakably Japanese, for in place of the soft, relaxed forms of Chinese Buddhist sculpture it has a Japanese taut, upright outline. Like much Japanese art it is basically linear in conception.

81.

81.
HEAD OF A HEAVENLY KING (*LOKAPALA*)
Late Heian Period, A.D. 12th century
Japan
wood
h: 11 1/4 in., w: 7 in., d: 6 7/8 in.
The Eugene and Margaret McDermott Fund
1982.8.McD

Another type of Buddhist figure in Japanese art is the Guardian King, or Lokapala, who protects the Buddhist faith from demonic onslaughts. Such guardian spirits are usually shown as ferocious, menacing warriors. This forceful imagery gives full rein to the Japanese taste for charged outlines and dramatic power. Since Japan was dominated by aristocratic warriors, it is not surprising to find a warlike ethos in its art.

The Museum's Lokapala sculpture consists only of the head from a full-length wooden guardian figure designed to be placed by the entrance to a shrine or temple. The powerfully muscular face has affinities with early Japanese dance masks and is carved in linear patterns which articulate the head as an image of benevolent ferocity.

83.

82.

84.

82.
MONJU
Nanbokucho Period, A.D.1331-1391
Japan
hanging scroll, colors on silk
with *kirikane* technique
h: 39 3/4 in., w: 16 1/2 in.
Dallas Art Association purchase
1970.8

The type of Buddhism popular in China and Japan is known as Mahayana Buddhism. It presented a more miraculous and supernatural character than the simple, humanist doctrines of early Buddhism. A Japanese hanging scroll represents Manjusri, one of the early followers of the Buddha, who became an important Bodhisattva in Mahayana belief. His merit could bring salvation to sinful men.

The impressive 14th-century painting shows Manjusri, or Monju as he was called in Japan, as a divine child riding on a lion. He carries a lotus flower upholding the Buddhist scriptures and a sword to strike down ignorance. Like the Lokapala figure, the image of Monju is distinctly militant. The innocent child and the ferocious lion appear to surge forward from the picture plane. The brilliant crimson and green colors, highlighted by cut gold decoration, and the intricate, sharply cut outlines suggest supernatural force. Japanese artists were masters of two-dimensional patterning. They did not attempt a plastic effect, but created calligraphic patterns on the flat surface of a painting. Monju is a bright iconic image.

83.
Detail from one of a pair of two-fold screens entitled
SCENES FROM ''TALES OF ISE''
Tosa Mitsuyoshi, (Japanese, 1539-1613)
ink, color, and gold on paper
h: 64 in., w: 37 1/8 in. (each leaf)
Gift of the Alvin and Lucy Owsley Foundation
1971.96

The same two-dimensional decorative sense may be seen in this 16th-century screen which illustrates a story from an old collection of fables, the *Tales of Ise*. The story is a romantic tale of two lovers who have eloped together; they are awaiting the moment when the people who are pursuing them will fire the grass in which they are hiding and discover them.

The drama of this scene is not conveyed by strong expressions or realistic details. In fact, the doomed couple appears completely expressionless. It is the vast, all-encompassing loneliness of the empty gold screen and the tense lines of waving grass which convey, through pattern alone, the tragic dimension of the lovers' fate. The art of screen decoration is allusive rather than narrative.

84.
CUP
Nabeshima, A.D. 17th century
Japan
porcelain, underglaze blue
h: 3 1/2 in., w: 2 5/16 in., d: 1 27/32 in.
Gift of Mr. and Mrs. Richard D. Haynes
1982.34

While Japanese ceramics do not have the range and technical virtuosity of Chinese works, they are miracles of subtle design. This 17th-century cup from the Nabeshima kilns has a most elegant oval, curving form, referred to as a ''Chinese bell flower'' shape. Its cobalt blue underglaze has a reserve design of poppy heads, which trail gracefully around the cup. As in China, fine porcelains were made to be treasured and admired as works of art, or even works to inspire thoughtful meditation, rather than simply being considered articles of use.

85.

86.

85.
KANZAN
86.
JITTOKU
Pair of hanging scrolls
Soga Shōhaku, (Japanese, 1730-1783)
sumi ink on paper
h: 49 1/8 in., w: 21 3/8 in. (each)
Gift of Mr. and Mrs. Lawrence S. Pollock
1970.28 and 1970.29

Buddhism was expressed in a variety of forms in Japan, perhaps the most important for art being the tradition of Zen. Zen Buddhism is a way of directly perceiving universal Reality and of achieving Enlightenment through intuitive vision. From the 15th century on, some of the most distinctive Japanese arts, including the tea ceremony, swordsmanship, *sumi* ink painting and *haiku* poetry, were practiced by devotees of Zen. Being by nature non-verbal and non-rational, Zen ways of seeing led to sensitive and subtle art forms. Ink painting, which attempted to catch the essence of a subject in a few graphic lines, was a natural expression of Zen's unmediated vision.

The pair of hanging scrolls representing Kanzan and Jittoku are examples of the condensed style found in black and white ink painting. The two men were a pair of mad monks who spoke a private language to each other while ignoring the everyday world. The Zen rejection of logic and tradition is symbolized by Jittoku's broom, which sweeps away reasoning, and Kanzan's blank scroll, which is empty of scriptures. In a few bold sweeps of the brush the pair of cosmic clowns, grotesque and yet inspired, are delineated as sacred figures. They are complements of each other, like the two halves of a sphere. The artist, Soga Shōhaku, was himself a member of a Zen family, whose traditions he has here distilled.

87.

87.
TIGER
after 1792
Nagasawa Rosetsu, (Japanese, 1755-1799)
ink and pigment on paper
h: 50 3/8 in., w: 11 1/8 in.
Dallas Museum of Fine Arts purchase
1972.13

The painting of a tiger by the eccentric artist Nagasawa
Rosetsu has the same economy of effect. The inscription on the scroll indicates that the artist was able to
express the essential nature of "tiger" without painting the whole animal. The Japanese feeling for subtly
allusive design is here brilliantly exemplified, as the
front part of the tiger strides forward on big, soft,
menacing paws. The twisting tip of the tiger's tail
spirals upward to the inscription in the upper part of
the picture. In its balance of empty and filled space
and its decorative placement of asymmetric forms,
the painting is very characteristic of Japanese patterning. The tiger is both funny and ferocious, recalling the divine madness of Kanzan and Jittoku.

88.
IRIS AND MANDARIN DUCKS
Sakai Hoitsu, (Japanese, 1761-1828)
ink and pigment on silk
h: 51 in., w: 22 3/16 in.
Foundation for the Arts Collection,
gift of Mr. and Mrs. Stephen S. Kahn
1972.7.FA

Sakai Hoitsu was a Buddhist monk of distinguished
family who painted numerous works in an eclectic
style. One of his most important themes was a series
of seasonal paintings, of which the Museum's scroll is
an example. Two mandarin ducks, symbols of married fidelity, sit on a stone beneath a clump of swamp
iris. The painting has the same asymmetric design as
Rosetsu's tiger, in which an empty left side of the
picture is balanced by a filled right side. There is no
illusion of depth.

The background is neutral, suggesting the universal
background of Nature, which underlies all life. A few
spots of brilliant color, such as the dark purple iris
flowers, add intensity to the muted painting. The
brushwork is very soft, dissolving into the silk in broad
washes, yet is completely controlled. It is a gentle
and peaceful picture of harmonious nature, made vital
by the pure lines and by the springing swords of the
iris leaves.

88.

VIII.

Ancient Mediterranean Art

The origins of European art lie in the various art traditions which developed in the eastern Mediterranean area beginning in the Neolithic period. High civilizations, characterized by the development of writing and monumental architecture, appeared in both Egypt and Mesopotamia by 3000 B.C. Here are the roots of classical Greek art, a tradition which, by way of Rome, was to mold the character of European culture. Here religious art, found in every early civilization, was transformed by the idea of humanism.

89.

90.

89.
OXEN AND WAGON
Proto-Hittite, 2000-1800 B.C.
Asia Minor
bronze
h: 6 9/16 in. (wagon), l: 21 3/4 in. (overall)
The Irvin L. and Meryl P. Levy Endowment Fund
1972.38

One of the important early empires in the Near East was that of the Hittites. Their kingdom, centered in eastern Anatolia, was notable for advances in metallurgy and technology. The bronze group of a wagon drawn by oxen was perhaps an offering in a shrine or tomb. Its stylized naturalism has a fine clarity of outline and a crisp simplicity. A great deal of Near Eastern art was devoted to animals, which were so vital to a hunting and farming way of life. This group suggests the creaking vehicle, mounted on the solid, spokeless wooden circles which were the first wheels, that in the dawn of wheeled transport would have lumbered slowly forward, drawn by oxen.

90.
THOTH, GOD OF LEARNING
AND PATRON OF SCRIBES
26th Dynasty, 663-525 B.C.
Egyptian
slate
h: 14 3/8 in., w: 4 3/4 in.
Gift of Elsa von Seggern
1979.1

In Egypt the growth of a unified kingdom under the rule of the Pharaoh meant extensive patronage of the arts. For centuries the great temple complexes of Egypt acted as administrators for the royal court. Kings, nobles and priests commissioned many works to ornament palaces and temples for the living and to furnish the tombs of the dead. Schools of trained artists existed to satisfy this demand.

Although the Museum's slate relief is from a late period of Egyptian art, it has the hieroglyphic purity of an earlier Egyptian style. Egyptian art was very conservative; once a satisfactory visual convention had been created, it might last for generations. The image of Thoth, god of learning, is carved in sunk relief. The ibis-headed god strides forward in the conventional posture designed for processional reliefs. The relief, which probably decorated a throne, is sharply cut for maximum readability; inscription and image are united.

94

91.
STANDING WOMAN, HORSE,
AND TWO DEITY FIGURES
Archaic Boeotian, 6th century B.C.
Greece
ceramic, paint
h: 6 3/4 in. (left figure)
Foundation for the Arts Collection,
gift of Mr. and Mrs. James H. Clark
1974.86.FA, 1974.90.FA, 1974.88.FA, 1974.87.FA

In all ancient civilizations, offering figures were common. They were prayers for health or good luck, or thanksgiving offerings for good fortune, which a worshipper could leave for the god or goddess he venerated. Shrines and temples were regularly given such offerings, which might be displayed for a time and then buried. People might also have such figures in their home or family shrines. Some were left in tombs.

A large number of such clay offering figures exists from the early periods of Greek art. Often, like this group of figurines, they refer to the cult of the Mother Goddess Demeter and her daughter, Persephone, who represented the rebirth of life in the springtime. These little moldmade figures are modest in scope, as they were not intended to be expensive, but they demonstrate the skills of Greek potters, who could produce charming works for large-scale production.

91.

92.

92.
FEMALE FIGURES IN BREAST-PRESENTING POSTURE
left to right:
Luba
Africa, Zaire
ivory
h: 3 1/2 in., w: 1 7/32 in., d: 1 1/4in.
Hacilar, 6th-5th millenium B.C.
Turkey, Anatolia
ceramic, paint, obsidian
h: 6 in., w: 2 13/16 in., d: 1 7/16 in.
Susa, 1200-900 B.C.
Iran
ceramic
h: 7 1/2 in., w: 2 5/8 in., d: 1 3/64 in.
Luristan, 1000-650 B.C.
Iran
bronze
h: 5 5/8 in., w: 13/16 in., d: 1 3/16 in.
Phoenician (?), c.1000 B.C.
Syria
bronze
h: 6 7/32 in., w: 1 1/4 in., d:1 1/32 in.
Michoacan, 300-100 B.C.
Mexico
ceramic
h: 3 7/8 in., w: 1 3/8 in., d: 9/16 in.
Foundation for the Arts Collection,
the Mr. and Mrs. Stanley Marcus Collection of Fertility Figures
1982.367.FA, 1982.308.FA, 1982.338.FA, 1982.333.FA, 1982.328.FA,
1982.382.FA

93.
GROUP OF FEMALE FIGURES
Mossi
Africa, Upper Volta
wood, leather, metal, cowry shells
h: 19 1/8 in. (largest figure)
Foundation for the Arts Collection,
the Mr. and Mrs. Stanley Marcus Collection of Fertility Figures
1982.348.FA, 1982.352.FA, 1982.349.FA, 1982.353.FA, 1982.351.FA,
1982.347.FA, 1982.350.FA

A related group of art works from the Mr. and Mrs. Stanley Marcus Collection of Fertility Figures, includes examples of similar offertory objects from all over the world. The image of woman as mother and source of human fertility appears in virtually all cultures; this collection makes it possible to trace the theme cross-culturally. Often the same form, such as a nude woman holding out her breasts, occurs in societies with no historical connections. These figurines are interesting examples of the fact that art expresses universal human realities. The collection is an ideal complement to the general Museum collections, which also demonstrate the unity in variety to be found in world art.

93.

94.

94.
BLACK-FIGURE TRIPOD *KOTHON*
c. 570 B.C.
Greek, Boeotian
terra cotta
h: 5 3/8 in., dia: 7 1/4 in.
Anonymous gift in memory of Edward S. Marcus
1981.170

Painted pottery was produced in large numbers in Greece during the 6th century B.C., both for local use and for exports. This demand led, as in China, to fertile invention in both pottery form and painted scenes. The unusual shape of this vessel, called a kothon, was probably due to its purpose as a scent container, but its firmly constructed, almost architectural design is representative of Greek ceramics. Greek pots have the character of small buildings.

The decoration of the vase is black figure, which means that the figures are painted on the body of a vessel in a fine slip that turns black during firing and stands out against the lighter color of the clay. In the first half of the 6th century ceramic decoration often took the form of an overall pattern such as you see on the kothon. There is a tapestry-like blend of heraldic panthers, *komasts* (or satyr-dancers) and geometric details. The ornamental effect of this decorative style has a delightful appeal.

95.
BLACK-FIGURE KYLIX
6th century B.C.
Of the circle of the Lysippides painter
Greek: Attic
terra cotta
h: 4 5/8 in., w: 16 1/8in. (with handles)
Gift of Mr. and Mrs. Cecil H. Green
1972.5

Greek pottery was thrown on the potter's wheel, allowed to dry to a leather-hard condition, and then painted freehand. The precision and finesse of draughtsmanship on these vases is as amazing as the quality of many of the painted scenes. Although Greek ceramics were completely different in character from Chinese ceramics, they represent a comparable genius. In Greek design there is no question of glazes; the shiny quality of the painted decorations is mainly due to the nature of the clay slips used as paints. These are not vitreous, like true glazes, but they have a slick surface after firing. It is the architectonic abilities of both potter and vase painter (usually different people) which give the finest Greek vases their remarkable splendor of design.

All of these features may be seen in the Museum's black figure kylix, or wine cup. The cup itself is splendidly articulated, in clean sweeping lines. The ornamental details and defining bands of paint have a masterly precision, animated by the clusters of grape leaves and grapes under the handles. The design is dominated by two large eyes, which were intended to ward off evil (and possibly drunkenness) from the person using the cup. Inside the cup is a Medusa head, or gorgoneion, which served the same purpose. On each side of the bowl is a vignette of the demi-god Herakles, who drinks or draws his sword. The fascination of Greek artists with observable reality may be seen in the careful depiction of Herakles' anatomy and drapery, and the crystalline drawing of his weapons and lion skin.

95.

96.
BLACK-FIGURE PANEL AMPHORA
6th century B.C.
Painter of the Medea Group
Greek: Attic
terra cotta
h: 18 1/4in., dia: 11 in.
Munger Fund purchase
1965.29

Throughout the 6th century B.C. Greek pottery paint-ers experimented with ways to describe reality on the curved surface of a vase. In the best examples, the urge toward description is balanced by the necessity of creating an effective two-dimensional design. For instance, this stately amphora has two panel scenes representing combats from the Trojan War. The heroic ethos attributed to the contestants in this war appears first in Homer's *Illiad*, a fountainhead of Greek civilization. The amphora depicts scenes in which the Greek hero Achilles and the African Prince Memnon, who was fighting on the Trojan side, contest the body of the dead Antilochus. Combat here is frozen in a central heraldic group which maintains the nature of the vessel in its flat pattern. To either side of the heroes are their mothers, mourning a battle which can only end in loss for one of them. The scene is both ornamental and filled with a sense of tragedy; it is purely humanistic, without any scenic distraction from the confrontation of armed warriors, one of whom must die.

97. *illustration on page 92*
FIGURE OF A YOUNG MAN
FROM A FUNERARY RELIEF
c. 330 B.C.
Greek: Attic
marble
h: 63 1/2 in., w: 30 3/4 in., d: 18 3/4 in.
Gift of Mr. and Mrs. Cecil H. Green
1966.26

This heroic ideal, with its tragic undertones, is even more splendidly embodied in the 4th-century B.C. marble statue of a young man from a funerary monument. It is one of the very few Greek originals of high quality from this period. The man for whom the statue was commissioned probably fell in one of the wars of the late 4th century — perhaps in one of Alexander the Great's battles. However, even if the

head of the figure and the rest of the relief were intact, it would not be a realistic portrait, but rather an idealized and timeless image, characteristic of clas-sical Greek art. The young man is shown as a beauti-ful nude athlete figure embodying the highest Greek values, which centered on human perfection. The fig-ure is sumptuously modelled, in a style apparently realistic but actually highly stylized, with pure, grace-ful forms and contrapuntal rhythms. Timeless beauty is not the only element of the sculpture; there is the intimation of mortality, an underlying sense of death and tragic loss, which gives deep meaning to the calm forms of Greek classicism.

98.
HEAD FROM AN ANTEFIX
c. 500 B.C.
Etruscan
painted terra cotta
h: 8 31/32 in., w: 5 5/8 in., d: 5 3/16 in.
Foundation for the Arts Collection,
anonymous gift in honor of Melba D. Whatley
1982.93.FA

The Etruscans, a people of still mysterious background, founded a number of kingdoms in north central Italy which, from the 6th century B.C. on, were the source of many art works based on Greek style. Greek ceram-ics and bronzes were imported into Etruria; these were later to be rediscovered in Etruscan tombs. In addition, Etruscan artists imitated or adapted Greek art, often with a strong native cast of character. In one way, then, Etruscan art is a provincial Greek art, while in another it is a fascinating new creation.

An example of this process is the terra cotta antefix dating to the early 5th century. This kind of architec-tural decoration would have been placed along the eaves of an Etruscan temple. The style of the female head originated in Archaic Greek art, with its stylized features and enigmatic smile. The bold simplifications and coloristic effect of the head are Etruscan.

99.
AMPHORA
6th century B.C.
Etruscan
terra cotta
h: 14 1/2 in., dia: 11 1/8 in.
Gift of Mr. and Mrs. Cecil H. Green
1966.23

Just as the antefix head simplifies Greek style, this vase adapts the style of East Greek ceramics to a native Etruscan taste for soft shapes and sensual, expressionistic effects. The crispness of outline and strong light/ dark contrasts of Greek vase paintings have been abandoned in favor of matte earth tones, textural hatching and elongated line. The hard intellectual clarity of Greek design is replaced by a sensuous romanticism.

100.
FUNERARY EARRINGS
4th-3rd century B.C.
Etruscan
gold
h: 4 7/8 in., w: 2 5/8 in. (left)
h: 4 13/16 in., w: 2 21/32 in. (right)
Gift of Mr. and Mrs. Cecil H. Green
1966.25. a and b

The Etruscans were expert metallurgists and jewelers. Rich ornaments like these massive, if lightweight, gold earrings have been found in Etruscan tombs and are also represented in funerary statues of Etruscan women. The earrings are miniature sculptures of considerable intricacy, as they combine the techniques of repoussé, filigree and granulation. The basic design of large bosses and smaller clusters of grapes is additionally ornamented by a central Medusa mask and the faces of three youths.

99.

100.

101.

101.
HEAD OF A YOUNG MAN
A.D. 100-130
Roman
marble
h: 8 7/8 in., w: 6 1/2 in.
Anonymous gift in memory of Edward S. Marcus
1981.169

By the 1st century B.C. the city of Rome had become the center of a vast empire covering the entire Mediterranean world. Like the Etruscans before them, the Romans admired Greek art. Following their conquest of the Greek states, they carried off many Greek art treasures to Italy and also employed Greek artists to work for them. The practical and puritanical Romans had different tastes from the Greeks, however, and gradually a new, Roman style developed under the Roman Empire.

One of the distinctive forms of Roman art was realistic portraiture, which was in keeping with Roman interest in history and in family lineage. Instead of the idealized forms of Greek art, Roman portraits have a strong sense of psychological reality. They were often quite unflattering. This head of a young man from the 2nd century A.D. reveals a rather spoilt, self-indulgent person. The modelling and carving are very skillful, which adds to the ambiguous effect of the portrait.

102.
FIGURE OF A WOMAN
A.D. 2nd century
Roman
marble
h: 69 1/4 in., w: 28 1/4 in., d: 17 5/8 in.
Gift of Mr. and Mrs. Cecil H. Green
1973.11

The way in which artists during the Roman Empire transformed older conventions of Greek art may be seen in the Museum's impressive funerary statue of a Roman lady. The body of the figure, which was made separately from the head, belongs to a type of Greek sculpture dating to the 4th century B.C. By the time this sculpture was created in the 2nd century A.D., the heavily draped figure was used as a conventional image of classic dignity. The woman's head, on the other hand, is a portrait of an actual woman.

The composite statue pictures a virtuous Roman matron of distinguished family, a chaste wife and mother of children. Marriage was one of the basic symbols of Roman life. Roman women, unlike Greek women, had force, personality and an important position in the Roman world. In a statue like this, the idealization of Greek art has been joined to the historical reality of Roman art to produce a symbol of marriage as an enduring value.

102.

109.

IX.

European Art: 17th-18th Centuries

The Museum has very few works of medieval or Renaissance European art. Examples of European art on display in the galleries primarily begin at the turn of the 16th and 17th centuries, with the origins of Baroque art. Two interesting proto-Baroque Italian painters, Pietro Paolini and Giulio Cesare Procaccini, are represented by a mythological and a religious work respectively. In these paintings one sees the classical, humanist side of Renaissance art and the Catholic iconography of the Counter-Reformation: the two symbolic value systems that were to dominate European art for centuries.

103.
Giulio Cesare Procaccini (Italian, 1574-1625)
ECCE HOMO
after 1615
oil on canvas
h: 92 5/8 in., w: 65 3/8 in.
Gift of Mr. and Mrs. Algur H. Meadows
and the Meadows Foundation, Incorporated
1969.16

The Milanese artist Giulio Cesare Procaccini painted in a style still close to the Mannerist tradition of Late Renaissance art. In his *Ecce Homo,* the severely flattened spatial composition, which gives the effect of a relief sculpture, is Mannerist in origin. The figures and the architectural forms of the painting are so tightly packed into one plane, as to scarcely suggest spatial depth at all. This effect is highly theatrical: the luminous white body of Christ, twisted in *contraposto* agony, stands out before the mocking figures of his tormentors. This powerful emotional impact, which causes the spectator to identify with the sufferings of Christ, is typical of Baroque art, and is achieved by a formal contrast between the ideal, nude figure of Christ and the realistic figures of uncomprehending mankind, who gesture crudely around Him.

103.

104.

104.
Pietro Paolini (Italian, 1603-1681)
BACCHIC CONCERT
c. 1625-30
oil on canvas
h: 46 in., w: 68 1/2 in.
Lent by the Hoblitzelle Foundation
97.1937

105.
Antonio de Pereda (Spanish, 1611-1678)
THE SACRIFICE OF ISAAC
c.1659
oil on canvas
h: 85 1/8 in., w: 67 1/4 in.
Lent by the Hoblitzelle Foundation
96.1937

Pietro Paolini was influenced in his development by the revolutionary art of Michelangelo Caravaggio. His *Bacchic Concert* has the ambiguous realism, pulsing with sensuality, which was Caravaggio's legacy to Baroque art. The theme of the painting, the wine god Bacchus and his followers, forms an interesting connection with the Museum's Classical collection, especially in the nude figure of the vine-crowned Bacchus. While the other figures in the scene are depicted in realistically rendered contemporary costume, the finely modelled nude torso of Bacchus has a startling erotic power. All of the textures in the painting — linen, brocade, flesh, flowers, bunches of grapes and wooden lute — are rendered in sumptuous chiaroscuro. The figures glow in mellow tones of tan, rust, cream and golden brown, with strongly marked highlights. Paolini injects the Dionysiac sensuality of the pagan world into an otherwise contemporary scene.

While both the Procaccini and the Paolini paintings are complex works, densely crowding figures to achieve dramatic intensity, the 17th century Spanish painter Antonio de Pereda presents a much simpler composition. The Biblical story of the sacrifice of Isaac by Abraham is illustrated only by the two frontal figures of father and son, which are fully and realistically modelled. Despite the attention to details of anatomy and clothing, the painting is idealized, for there is no sense of tragic suffering, only a willing acceptance of the mystic sacrifice. This was of theological importance, as Abraham's willingness to sacrifice his son was believed to prefigure God's gift of His son, Jesus. The contrast between the rugged figure of the aged Abraham and the soft, youthful beauty of Isaac adds to this religious meaning, for both participants seem in absolute submission to God's will.

105.

106.

106.
Osias Beert, the Elder (Flemish, c. 1580-1624)
BASKET OF FLOWERS
c.1615
oil on panel
h: 19 7/8 in., w: 25 7/8 in.
Munger Fund
1977.33.M

The realistic descriptions of anatomy and clothing in *The Sacrifice of Isaac,* which were subordinated to the demands of Spanish religious art, are only a part of a much wider interest in realism in the 17th century. The perspective illusionism of Renaissance art made it possible to represent the appearance of objects with minute fidelity. North European art, especially, was devoted to depicting observed reality for its own sake, in still life or genre scene.

The Flemish artist Osias Beert, who was one of the earliest painters of still life as an independent subject, created paintings notable for an almost hallucinatory sense of reality. In this work, the flowers — carnation, lily, tulip, iris, jonquil, phlox and peony — are shown with an absolute precision of detail, which is extended to the texture of the woven basket and to the fallen petals and slug, the debris of the flower arrangement. As is often the case in a North European still life, the picture hints at the transitoriness of sensuous experience, while embodying that experience in as physically brilliant a way as possible. The flowers glow with a dazzling luminosity of color and light.

107.
Barent Fabritius (Dutch, 1624-1673)
YOUNG GIRL PLUCKING A DUCK
c.1645
oil on canvas
h: 33 1/8 in., w: 27 9/16 in.
Anonymous gift
1963.149

"Realism" in European art is, on the one hand, a series of technical skills in perspective and figure modelling developed during the Renaissance, and, on the other, the stylistic use any particular artist may make of realistic description in painting. It has no meaning in itself, even in so illusionistic a work as Beert's still life. Barent Fabritius, a pupil of Rembrandt, takes an altogether different attitude toward realism in his painting of a young girl plucking a duck. The girl, whose youthful features are sensitively rendered, was Rembrandt's housekeeper. Although the subject is very mundane, the treatment of the scene is softly and luminously painted, giving both the girl and her work a quiet intensity. The background is sketchy and shadowy, making the scene more a portrait than a narrative. Fabritius had mastered Rembrandt's manner, if not his psychological power.

108.
Michael Sweerts (Flemish, 1624-1664)
PORTRAIT OF A YOUNG OFFICER
c.1646-52
oil on canvas
h: 38 1/2 in., w: 29 in.
Lent by the Hoblitzelle Foundation
11.1968

Fabritius' painting may be compared with another representation of an actual person, Michael Sweerts' *Portrait of a Young Officer.* This painting, too, shows a single figure against a dark, spatially undefined background, but in place of the young girl, of lower-class origins and unformed character, there is the opulent image of a well-to-do, self-confident young man of good birth. His stance and the position of his hands show he is born to command. Here, the resources of realism are devoted to rendering as clearly as possible the rich textures of the young man's fine clothes and gilt sword belt and his handsome, well-bred features. An assured technique is in the service of an aristocratic image.

110

107.

108.

109.	*illustration on page 106*
Nicolas Mignard (French, 1606-1668)
THE SHEPHERD FAUSTULUS
BRINGING ROMULUS AND REMUS TO HIS WIFE
1654
oil on canvas
h: 59 1/4 in., w: 57 1/2 in.
Gift of Mr. and Mrs. Algur H. Meadows
and the Meadows Foundation, Incorporated
1970.25

Art painted for the 17th century European upper class usually had this element of aristocratic display, but in a great monarchy, like the France of Louis XIV, it took the form of classic idealization. In *The Shepherd Faustulus Bringing Romulus and Remus to his Wife,* Nicolas Mignard paints a subject from Roman mythology in an ideal way, which demonstrates the value Greco-Roman culture had for cultivated Frenchmen in his time. His art is closely related to the classical paintings of Nicolas Poussin. In this scene, the fable of the twins Romulus and Remus, who were suckled by a she wolf, raised by a shepherd family, and survived to found the city of Rome, is given a timeless nobility. The figures are so clean as to seem modelled in marble. The colors are bright, primary reds and blues. Although both the shepherd's hut and the people in the scene are illusionistic, the overall effect of the painting is like a classical bas-relief. This idealization gives a rich, Vergilian dignity to characters who are actually poor peasants. It is Arcadia, not the true shepherd's hovel.

110.

110.
Claude-Joseph Vernet (French, 1714-1789)
MOUNTAIN LANDSCAPE WITH
AN APPROACHING STORM
1775
oil on canvas
h: 64 1/8 in., w: 102 3/4 in.
Foundation for the Arts Collection,
Mrs. John B. O'Hara Fund
1983.41.FA

The 18th century painter Claude-Joseph Vernet's vast landscape of a Mediterranean mountain scene has its roots in this idealizing classical tradition, particularly in the landscapes of Claude Lorrain. By the last half of the 18th century, however, an artist like Vernet was striving for effects of picturesque drama and naturalism alien to classical style. His successful career as one of the most prominent landscape painters of his time led him to create numerous views, which were both illustrations of the Mediterranean countries vis-

ited by noblemen on their Grand Tour of Europe and also attempts to appeal to the increasing taste for emotional and romantic feeling in art. In the broad scale and sweeping drama of this storm-lit mountain scene, Vernet goes beyond the ideal calm of 17th-century landscapes and anticipates the storm and stress of Romantic art, where landscape became an aspect of the Sublime. The thundering waterfall, rugged rocky coast and gusty storm clouds were romantic in inspiration, though painted with meticulous detail. Such grandiose compositions were still created for aristocratic patrons; this scene was commissioned by the Marquis of Lansdowne. Despite its overtures to Romanticism, the grandeur and elegance of the painting marks an art meant to appeal to the cultivated taste of people sharing a common cultural heritage.

111.
Jean-Baptiste Greuze (French, 1725-1805)
PORTRAIT OF JEAN-NICOLAS BILLAUD-VARENNE
early 1790s
oil on panel
h: 23 1/4 in., w: 19 1/4 in.
Gift of an anonymous foundation
1961.105

By the last half of the 18th century, this assured belief
in an aristocratic society, whose culture was derived
from Christianity and from the Greco-Roman world,
had been radically questioned. The Enlightenment in
France challenged traditional ideas and a hierarchic
social order. Eventually such criticism of the established order would lead to the French Revolution and
the deposition of the monarchy. Jean-Baptiste Greuze
was an artist whose work exemplified the increasing
emphasis on middle class sentiment and revolutionary ideas. His genre scenes, often filled with moraliz-
ing overtones, are illustrations of the way educated
people in 18th century France were rejecting the lax
habits of the old regime. A most accomplished painter,
his portrait of Jean-Nicolas Billaud-Varenne, an ardent
Republican during the early stages of the French
Revolution, catches the moral earnestness of the time.
It was such men as Billaud-Varenne, intellectually committed to the 18th century idea of Progress, who
brought about the Revolution. The masterly ease with
which the portrait is painted is matched only by the
gripping psychological penetration with which Greuze
envisions the stern man who would help make history.

111.

118.

X.

European Art: 19th Century

The complete upheaval in European society caused by the French Revolution and the Napoleonic Empire was accompanied in art by a shift from Classicism to Romanticism. A brief view of the great French Romantic painter, Eugène Delacroix, may be seen in the Museum's Delacroix drawing for *The Justice of Trajan,* illustrated in Chapter 16. Perhaps even more important than the Romantic impulse was the slow, but steady, movement from a Christian, aristocratic culture to a secular and democratic one. This movement created the conditions of the modern world.

112.
Honoré Daumier (French, 1808-1879)
OUTSIDE THE PRINT-SELLER'S SHOP
c.1860-63
oil on panel
h: 13 1/16 in., w: 9 1/2 in.
Foundation for the Arts Collection,
Mrs. John B. O'Hara Fund
1981.33.FA

One of the important artists who registered the uneasy progress toward a commercial, secular society was Honoré Daumier. The larger part of Daumier's output was his satiric graphics, but he was also a fine painter. His oil paintings have a deep humanism, for which there is little scope in his prints, since they pinpoint the weaknesses of an emerging capitalist civilization. *Outside the Print-Seller's Shop* is a subject which might be treated sardonically in a print, but the oil painting has an accepting wisdom worthy of Rembrandt. Anonymous people — a rather seedy professional man, a woman, a poor person, a child — peer earnestly and innocently at the kind of art available to the passerby, or they ignore it. The meeting of the City and Art have rarely been grasped in so brief and poignant a compass.

112.

113.
Gustave Courbet (French, 1819-1877)
FOX IN THE SNOW
1860
oil on canvas
h: 33 3/4 in., w: 50 1/16 in.
Foundation for the Arts Collection,
Mrs. John B. O'Hara Fund
1979.7.FA

Daumier chose to approach the real world of Louis-Philippe's bourgeois monarchy or Napoleon III's Second Empire by way of satire. Gustave Courbet, with a militant enthusiasm characteristic of his powerful personality, directly assaulted the artistic and cultural Establishment of mid-19th century France, in a series of strongly realistic oil paintings. He used realism as a bludgeon in his war with conventional art.

Fox in the Snow is related to larger paintings Courbet executed on the subject of game and hunting. He was himseif a passionate huntsman. In theme, the work is a stark, unsentimental view of wild nature: the starving fox is greedily gnawing a small rat. In execution, the picture is a subtle view of a winter landscape, in which the bloody scraps of the victim echo the russet tips of the snow-covered herbage. All of the textures of the snow scene are finely rendered, but the central figure of the sleekly glowing fox has the painterly richness by means of which Courbet often surpassed his doctrinaire ideas about realism. Like the contemporary poet, Victor Hugo, Courbet thought of his work in terms of broad and powerful effects.

113.

116

114.

115.

114.
Jean-Louis-Ernest Meissonier (French, 1815-1891)
INFORMATION (GENERAL DESAIX AND
THE PEASANT)
1867
oil on panel
h: 12 7/16 in., w: 16 in.
Foundation for the Arts Collection,
Mrs. John B. O'Hara Fund
1978.55.FA

115.
Frédéric Bazille (French, 1841-1871)
PORTRAIT OF PAUL VERLAINE AS A TROUBADOUR
1868
oil on canvas
h: 18 1/16 in., w: 15 in.
Foundation for the Arts Collection,
Mrs. John B. O'Hara Fund
and a gift from Colonel C. Michael Paul
1978.68.FA

The bourgeois culture which Courbet opposed throughout his life had its own canons of art. The academic painter J.L.E. Meissonier made his reputation through meticulously realistic scenes, rendered in great detail. Under Napoleon III's Empire, he painted a number of scenes which glorified the campaigns of the elder Napoleon. These scenes have a narrative, illustrative character far removed from the broad, even coarse, realism of Courbet. Meissonier's paintings are highly finished and smooth, with no sense of the painter's brush. In *Information* a peasant gives critical information to a Napoleonic leader. General Desaix and the Old Guard appear impressive in a theatrical way, and, indeed, Meissonier researched their uniforms as a stage designer might for a play. The veristic rendering of the winter landscape and the uniformed men is an attempt, in the manner of an historical novel, to recreate the great days of Napoleon's victories.

A contrasting image from the artists who rejected the patronage of established culture, as they rejected its political ideology, is Frédéric Bazille's *Portrait of Paul Verlaine as a Troubadour*. Bazille was a friend of the Impressionists, who died at the untimely age of 29 during the Franco-Prussian War. He belonged to the circle of Manet, Monet and Degas and shared their innovative views of art. This romantic portrait presents the French Symbolist poet Paul Verlaine in the costume of a troubadour. An admiration for the past had always been an element in Romantic art. Verlaine's own poetry had an ambiguous relation with the past, as well as a synthesis of music and poetry symbolized by the medieval image of the troubador.

The portrait fuses Verlaine's metaphorical disguise with his thoughtful, sensitive face, which is realistically treated. Stylistically, Bazille's brief oeuvre falls between Realism and Impressionism, but this striking work is a kind of cultural icon for the avant-garde.

116.
Claude Monet (French, 1840-1926)
THE SEINE AT LAVACOURT
1880
oil on canvas
h: 38 3/4 in., w: 58 3/4 in.
Munger Fund
1938.4.M

Impressionism began as an extension of the efforts of artists like Courbet or the painters of the Barbizon School to open up the techniques and subject matter of painting and to escape the highly finished studio pictures exhibited at the French Salon of the Academy of Fine Arts. The first Impressionist painters were also affected by scientific advances, such as photography or the investigation of the nature of color and light. The Impressionists, however, appeared far more radical even than Courbet. When Claude Monet first exhibited his pictures, critics considered them incoherent and unfinished; ''Impressionism'' was used as an insulting term. Yet Monet's Impressionist vision only carried further the concern with representing visual reality on a two-dimensional canvas, which had preoccupied artists since the Renaissance.

The Seine at Lavacourt was painted during the period in the 1880s when Monet was living at Vetheuil. Here he painted the River Seine from the village of Lavacourt, on the opposite bank of the stream. This work has the recognizable characteristics of Monet's Impressionist style: a light ground, separate brush strokes, a white and pastel palette and forms which are dissolved into an overall web of paint. What chiefly concerned Monet was the effect of light on form; the vibrant shimmer of the painting is due to the manner in which Monet unified sky, water, trees and town into a single reflective pattern of blue-green and cream tones. Air, light and landscape become one.

117.
Claude Monet (French, 1840-1926)
WATER LILIES
1908
oil on canvas
dia: 31 1/2 in.
Gift of the Meadows Foundation, Incorporated
1981.128

This fascination with the way in which forms are dissolved in light, as well as the interplay of light and color, continued to be Monet's major concern until the end of his life. Where other Impressionist painters like Renoir and Pissarro turned to new stylistic interests, he remained an Impressionist painter, because the immediacy with which Impressionist technique could apprehend a scene suited his way of seeing. He always was concerned about the changing appearance of a scene at different times of day or in different weather; the sketchy forms and broken brushwork of Impressionism enabled him to seize these fleeting perceptions.

During his old age, when he was living at his country home near Giverny, Monet returned again and again to the theme of water lilies, painting the floating forms in the pond at the bottom of his garden. In such works Monet approached abstraction, for the forms of the lilies are barely defined and they blend into the blue, green and pink surface of the canvas. The sparkling light upon the still water of the pond seems to have embodied itself in shimmering tones. The art of appearance is replaced by the apprehension of a magic truth about light.

118

116.

117.

119

118. *illustration on page 114*
Edouard Manet (French, 1832-1883)
PORTRAIT OF ISABELLE LEMONNIER
c.1879
oil on canvas
h: 36 in., w: 28 3/4 in.
Gift of Mr. and Mrs. Algur H. Meadows
and the Meadows Foundation, Incorporated
1978.1

A similar effect of rapid brushwork and immediate grasp of the subject may be seen in Edouard Manet's *Portrait of Isabelle Lemonnier,* although Manet did not consider himself to be a close part of the Impressionist group. From the 1860s on, Manet had been one of the most innovative of French artists. His *Luncheon on the Grass* scandalized the Paris art world in 1863, laying the groundwork for the independent Impressionist exhibitons later. Despite the attacks of his critics, Manet continued to paint distinctive and elegant scenes of contemporary life, in a manner far removed from work done for the Salon.

His *Portrait of Isabelle Lemmonier* comes from the last years of his life; when the ageing artist was attracted to a dashing young girl. He painted Mlle. Lemmonier a number of times, treating her figure in a brilliantly summary way. The girl's prosperous appearance and strong personality are captured in broad patches of color and deft outlines. The oil painting has almost the effect of a drawing, revealing each stroke of the artist's hand with great immediacy.

119.
Berthe Morisot (French, 1841-1895)
WOMAN WITH A MUFF
1880
oil on canvas
h: 29 in., w: 23 in.
Gift of the Meadows Foundation Incorporated
1981.129

A comparable painting is Berthe Morisot's *Woman with a Muff.* Morisot was the daughter of a well-to-do official and a descendant of the painter Fragonard; from an early age she was attracted to a career in painting. She was a friend of the Impressionists and worked closely with Manet, whose brother she married. Her work shares with the other Impressionists an interest in the effects of light, rapid brushwork

and subjects chosen from contemporary life, but her style has a fresh lightness that is all her own. The Museum's painting is a good example of her very harmonious blending of tones: here, golds, browns and creams. The surface of the painting is alive with a vitality created by energetic brush work. The figure of the lady, caught in a momentary, turning pose, is unified with the hints of natural forms in the background by luminous golden tones.

119.

120.

120.
Camille Pissarro (French, 1830-1903)
APPLE PICKING AT ERAGNY-SUR-EPTE
1888
oil on canvas
h: 23 in., w: 28 1/2 in.
Munger Fund
1955.17.M

The Impressionists' use of separate brush strokes to convey the sparkle of air and light out of doors led to more radical experiments. Seurat and Signac originated a method called Pointillism, in which small strokes of pure color are applied to the canvas in a pattern of dots. The juxtaposed colors are fused by the viewer's eye. Camille Pissarro, who was one of the original Impressionist painters, experimented with this technique during the late 1870s and early 1880s.

Pissarro's *Apple Picking at Eragny-Sur-Epte* reflects this period in his art. A harvest scene of apple pickers is rendered in a pattern of gold, blue, rose and chartreuse brush strokes, forming a flat, two-dimensional design. The apple pickers are seen as colored silhouettes. This flat, brightly colored imagery anticipates the Post-Impressionist work of Van Gogh and Gauguin somewhat later. In the ornamental outdoor scene, there is no longer a sense of air and space, but rather a pattern in which all the forms, even the shadows, have bright coloristic power.

121.
Vincent Van Gogh (Dutch, 1853-1890)
RIVERBANK IN SPRINGTIME
1887
oil on canvas
h: 19 in., w: 22 1/4 in.
The Eugene and Margaret McDermott Fund
in memory of Arthur Berger
1961.99.McD

In 1886 Vincent Van Gogh left his native Holland to work in Paris, where he stayed until 1888. Here he saw work by Impressionist and Pointillist artists and began to paint in a different way from the work he had created earlier. The Museum's spring scene by a riverside belongs to this period, when Van Gogh was absorbing methods he found in the Parisian art world, including the use of light, white tones and separate brush strokes. While the painting has none of the emotional force characteristic of Van Gogh's later work in southern France, it is an interesting example of his efforts to expand his skills. It is gentle, peaceful and fresh, with the light of springtime on new green growth.

121.

122.

122

123.

122.
Paul Gauguin (French, 1848-1903)
I RARO TE OVIRI (UNDER THE PANDANUS)
1891
oil on canvas
h: 26 1/2 in., w: 35 1/2 in.
Foundation for the Arts Collection,
Adele R. Levy Fund
1963.58.FA

123.
Emile Bernard (French, 1868-1941)
BRETON WOMEN AT PRAYER
1892
oil on cardboard
h: 32 3/8 in., w: 45 3/4 in.
The Art Museum League Fund
1963.34

Van Gogh's friend, Paul Gauguin, was to make one of the critical moves in modern art, from an interest in the observable world, still present in Impressionism, to the idea of art as an abstract pattern, which was to dominate 20th century art. When he first began to paint, Gauguin was influenced by Pissarro; after he moved to the South Pacific, in 1891, his work was devoted to the kind of two-dimensional effects and simplified shapes with which he had begun to experiment while in Brittany in the late 1880s. *Under the Pandanus* was painted shortly after his move to Tahiti. It demonstrates Gauguin's continued fascination with the primitive life of the Polynesian villagers around him and the archetypal emotions they aroused in him. The scene is boldly painted, with a balance of flatly rendered figures and hot green and orange tones. At last, the Renaissance tradition of illusionism is abandoned in favor of decorative imagery of barbaric power.

When Gauguin was painting at Pont Aven in Brittany during the late 1880s, he met a young artist named Emile Bernard, whose Breton scenes shared with Gauguin's work an interest in decorative form. Bernard's delicate sensibility, however, is closer to Symbolist art, than to Gauguin's almost brutal dynamism. *Breton Women at Prayer* places a series of female figures in silhouette against a barely defined mass of trees. The shapes of the women, the trees, the shrubbery and the grass form a pattern without depth or perspective, which has connections with the Japanese prints so popular in France in the late 19th century.

125.

Jean-Baptiste Carpeaux (French, 1827-1875)
UGOLINO AND HIS CHILDREN
1860, cast c.1871
bronze
h: 19 in., w: 14 3/4 in., d: 10 5/8 in.
Foundation for the Arts Collection,
Mrs. John B. O'Hara Fund
1981.42.FA

In the Museum's 19th century sculpture collection, Romanticism is represented by a small-scale bronze version of J.B. Carpeaux's important work, *Ugolino and his Children*. Like Bazille's portrait of Paul Verlaine, Carpeaux's choice of subject reflected the Romantic love for the medieval past. Dante's *Divine Comedy* was a fertile source of dramatic subjects for artists throughout the century. Carpeaux began to develop the theme of Count Ugolino — who, after long imprisonment, starved to death, amidst the bodies of his children — while he was working in Italy during his *Prix De Rome* fellowship. The forms of the sculpture show the clear influence of Michelangelo, whose work Carpeaux had seen in Florence and Rome. Following Carpeaux's stay in Italy, the Ugolino sculpture was exhibited in Paris at the School of Fine Arts in 1861. *Ugolino and his Children* was not completely successful with the art critics of the Second Empire. Its terrible subject, and the harsh, contorted treatment of the nude figures, offended academic taste. On the other hand, the brilliant modelling and complex build-up of the composition were admired. Carpeaux's combination of technical facility and Romantic violence shows the range of creativity possible within the framework of official French art patronage.

Auguste Rodin (French, 1840-1917)
JEAN D'AIRE FROM THE BURGHERS OF CALAIS
by 1886 (plaster); cast early 20th century
bronze
h: 81 in., w: 28 in., d: 24 in.
Given in memory of Louie N. Bromberg and Mina Bromberg
by their sister Essie Bromberg Joseph
1981.1

Auguste Rodin, too, was influenced by Michelangelo, but his sculpture signified a break with academic art. Embodying his private passions in his sculptures, he was a Romantic in the inward sense, not as a matter

124.

126.

of fashion or style. His dramatic works, which fuse realism and a tormented consciousness, are true 19th century parallels to Michelangelo's titanic compositions. One of his greatest works was the group he designed for the city of Calais, on the historical theme of the Burghers of Calais. These medieval martyrs voluntarily offered their lives to the English King Edward III, to prevent him from sacking Calais after a siege. In Rodin's version of the subject, the six burghers are seen at the moment of grim self-sacrifice. There is no indication of the fact that the men were ultimately reprieved. Of the group of six, one of the most powerful figures is Jean d'Aire, who, in stark despair, carries the key of the city to present to the enemy king.

This sculpture is an early bronze casting of Rodin's nude study for Jean D'Aire. All of the figures in the group were created in nude models, preparatory to the final, clothed version. Rodin's wonderful sensitivity to the human figure may be seen in this study of a middle-aged man, his shoulders slumped in despair, his whole body rigid with stoic determination. The face is an image of anguished heroism, while the muscular body and splayed feet are expressionistic in their earthy power. Rodin's ability to infuse the physical substance of his sculptures with psychological force is embodied here in dramatic form.

126.
Edgar Degas (French, 1834-1917)
THE MASSEUSE
1896-1911
bronze
h: 16 1/4 in., w: 16 1/4 in., d: 14 in.
The Eugene and Margaret McDermott Fund
1965.26.McD

Edgar Degas, both in his sculptural modelling and in his painting, was concerned with the plastic and formal possibilities of people in movement. *The Masseuse,* like many other works, was cast, after Degas' death, in bronze from wax models left in his studio. These swift and brilliant works may have been intended as studies for his oil paintings, for the style of the models is similar to his drawings, while the subjects, such as bathers and dancers, are found in his paintings. *The Masseuse* is a dynamic composition, in which a dancer's body is being made limber by a *masseuse.* It is an unconventional composition, both in the momentary poses and in the fact that the group centers on open space between the two women, but it has, nevertheless, a very stable, even classical effect. Energy and stasis are in perfect balance. There are no distracting details; only Degas' swift economy in modelling the significant mass and line.

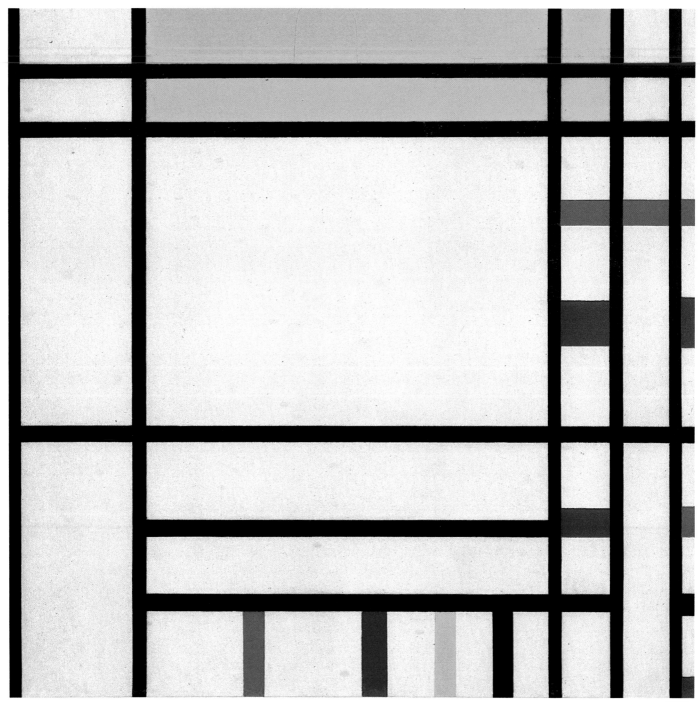

128b.

XI.

European Art: 20th Century

The development of modern art in Europe followed an unbroken line of growth, which built upon the experiments of Impressionism and Post-Impressionism. This is now seen as a move toward abstraction, but it is equally true that Cézanne, Gauguin and the Fauve painters were carrying on an investigation into the nature, structure and emotional character of painting, which goes back to the Renaissance concept of the artist as a conscious creator, playing, god-like, with his medium. The growth of Cubism meant the rejection of illusionism and three-dimensional appearance in painting, yet Picasso and Braque were in their own way classical, having an appreciation of geometric form the ancient Greeks might have shared.

127.

Painting

127.
Wassily Kandinsky (Russian, 1866-1944)
HOUSES IN MURNAU
1909-10
oil on paper mounted on masonite
h: 19 7/8 in., w: 25 in.
Dallas Art Association purchase
1963.31

Wassily Kandinsky, like Picasso, may be seen as a central figure in the creation of abstract art. The Museum's painting *Houses in Murnau* belongs to the critical years around 1910 when Kandinsky, a Russian living near Munich, began to approach pure abstraction. *Houses in Murnau* is still recognizable as a cityscape and it has elements found in the ornamental, flat patterning of Gauguin's work. The strong emotional effect formed by thickly painted patches of paint recollects the dynamic use of unrealistic color found in Fauve art, as well as the Expressionist effects of Kandinsky and his friends. Overall, however, the impression the painting gives is of Kandinsky pushing massive swathes of color here and there on the canvas, in abstract patterns. The scene is visualized as a harmony of brilliant shapes.

128.a.
Piet Mondrian (Dutch, 1872-1944)
BLUE TREE
c.1909-10
oil on composition board
h: 22 3/8 in. x w: 29 1/2 in.
Foundation for the Arts Collection,
gift of the James H. and Lillian Clark Foundation
1982.26.FA

The progression from expressive simplification of forms to pure abstraction occurs also in the work of the Dutch painter Piet Mondrian. Again, the Museum has a work from a critical point in Mondrian's art. In 1909 and 1910 Mondrian was working and reworking the image of trees, using a pattern of brush strokes owing something to Pointillism and Van Gogh, but chiefly concentrating on his own interest in structure. In *Blue Tree* the artist has reduced the tree form to a skeletal pattern of horizontal and vertical lines and the color is wholly unrealistic. The picture is an explosion of tense lines of energy, kept under rigid control. It is this control of material energy which Mondrian was to explore in his more completely abstract and linear works. Even here, line and pure color predominate.

128a.

128.b.   *illustration on page 126*
Piet Mondrian (Dutch, 1872-1944)
PLACE DE LA CONCORDE
1938-43
oil on canvas
h: 37 in., w: 37 3/16 in.
Dallas Museum of Fine Arts,
Foundation for the Arts Collection,
gift of the James H. and Lillian Clark Foundation
1982.22.FA.

By the early 1920s Mondrian had evolved his distinctive abstract style, which consisted of vertical and horizontal lines on a white ground, punctuated by blocks of primary colors. The Museum has several examples of Mondrian's work; *Blue Tree* may be compared with a late painting, *Place de la Concorde,* which represents a final summation of Mondrian's long creative effort to embody universal principles in an austere pictorial geometry. Beginning in the late 1930s and especially after Mondrian moved from Europe to New York in 1940, he was able to achieve a new level of artistic freedom, giving his later works a subtle dynamism and freer color rhythm that animates the restrained severity of his earlier rectilinear style. *Place de la Concorde* is fully representative of this development, with bright blocks of color that reverberate within the rigid black outlines. The tempo of the painting is lively and energetic, creating the tense, dynamic counterpoint of color and line which gives Mondrian's works their feeling of living force and power.

129.

129.
Liubov Popova (Russian, 1889-1924)
PAINTERLY ARCHITECTONICS
1918
oil on cardboard
h: 23 3/8 in., w: 15 1/2 in.
General Acquisitions Fund
and gifts from Mrs. Edward Marcus,
James H. Coker and Ann Addison,
Margaret Ann Bolinger, George and Schatzie Lee,
Mrs. Elizabeth B. Blake, and an anonymous donor
1982.10

At the time when Mondrian was first endeavoring to formulate a pure linear style, Russian Constructivist artists, stimulated by Cubism in France and Futurism in Italy, were engaged in an exuberant outburst of creative energy. The brief time between World War I and the early 1920s was one of revolutionary vigor in Russian avant-garde art circles. One of the leaders in Constructivist experimentation was Liubov Popova, a woman who had travelled extensively and whose paintings revealed a wide range of cultural and scientific interests. Her series of Painterly Architectonics resembles Cubism in its planar forms, but is filled with a remarkable dynamism and an open-ended force quite unlike the closed forms of Cubism. Asymmetric balance, irradiated by warm colors and glowing light, makes the painting seem like a cosmic explosion of forms.

130.
Fernand Léger (French, 1881-1955)
THREE WOMEN AND STILL-LIFE (DÉJEUNER)
1920
oil on canvas
h: 28 3/4 in., w 36 1/4 in.
Foundation for the Arts Collection,
gift of the James H. and Lillian Clark Foundation
1982.27.FA

Another example of a personal inspiration derived from Cubism is the work of Fernand Léger. Rarely is Léger's painting completely abstract; there are always references to the people and machines that stimulated his robust energy. During the 1920s, particularly, Léger created a series of monumental figures, whose multiple viewpoints and cylindrical forms recall Cubism, but whose ample volumes, dramatically related to a strong geometric background, are pure Léger. The Museum's *Three Women and Still Life* is an example of these neo-classic nudes of the machine age. There are echoes of earlier Impressionist art in the reclining women and the still life of a luncheon table, but the human intimacy of the scene is transformed into grandiose shapes, suitable for an industrial world.

131.
Robert Delaunay (French, 1885-1941)
EIFFEL TOWER
1924
oil on canvas
h: 72 1/2 in., w: 68 1/2 in.
Gift of the Meadows Foundation Incorporated
1981.105

Léger was attempting to find forms fitted to the dynamics of a changed way of life. In a series of paintings begun in 1910 and only ended in the 1920s, Robert Delaunay experimented with abstract scenes of the *Eiffel Tower,* as one of the main architectural images of modernism. *Eiffel Tower* combines a suggestion of the steel tower's elongated height, seen in a bird's eye view, with a basically flat composition of colored shapes. The triangle of the tower is completely integrated with the surface pattern of the streets at its base. The green/orange color complement, seen in Gauguin's *Under the Pandanus* and Popova's *Painterly Architectonics,* has become part of a bright symphony of saffron, purple and dark blue tones. Color in Delaunay's work has its own voice, while the geometric shapes are soft- edged and casually defined.

130.

131.

132.
Amedeo Modigliani (Italian, 1884-1920)
BOY IN SHORT PANTS
c.1918
oil on canvas
h: 39 1/2 in., w: 25 1/2 in.
Gift of the Leland Fikes Foundation, Inc.
1977.1

Delaunay's *Eiffel Tower* presents recognizable references to actual streets, traffic circles and buildings. Geometric abstraction was far from dominating all modern art; the possibilities opened up when the Post-Impressionists abandoned three dimensional illusionism could lead in many directions. Amadeo Modigliani devoted his short and troubled life to creating paintings, chiefly portraits of people he knew, treated in a flat, coolly modulated way. Often the faces of his portraits refer to the African masks which had fascinated several modern artists. *Boy in Short Pants,* with its acid yellow-green colors and air of remote detachment, has the ironic elegance which Modigliani often gave to his bohemian acquaintances.

133.

133.
George Rouault (French, 1871-1958)
THE ITALIAN WOMAN
1938
oil on panel
h: 31 1/4 in., w: 24 7/8 in.
Gift of Mr. and Mrs. Vladimir Horowitz
1976.53

A contrasting work is Georges Rouault's *The Italian Woman,* which has a dark, brooding intensity. The thick impasto and black defining lines recall Rouault's training as a stained glass designer, while the poetic feeling of the work, and the woman's air of quiet mystery, are part of the feeling for humanity so marked in Rouault's art. Without necessarily being directly religious, his subjects often have a spiritual dimension.

134.

134.
René Magritte (Belgian, 1898-1967)
THE LIGHT OF COINCIDENCES
1933
oil on canvas
h: 23 5/8 in., w: 28 3/4 in.
Gift of Mr. and Mrs. Jake L. Hamon
1981.9

Surrealism has proved to be one of the most important and long-lasting movements in 20th century art. The Museum has a major work by the Belgian Surrealist René Magritte, which exemplifies the variety latent in the original idea of Surrealism, that of freeing artistic creativity from the restraints of logic and reason. Appealing directly to dreams, automatic drawing or the unconscious mind, Surrealist artists like André Breton or Marcel Duchamp often juxtaposed unlikely objects to create meanings inexpressible in terms of straightforward visual reality. Since style in Surrealism depended on the individual artist's psyche, it was more a stimulus than a school. There are many types of Surrealist art. Magritte retained, in his subtly disturbing paintings, a workman-like Belgian craftsman's technique. He used the tricks of perspective illusionism to question the images created by them. In *The Light of Coincidences,* a three-dimensional painted box encloses the palpably real looking nude torso of a woman. This torso is lit by a candle, which is also a painted illusion. No element in the painting can be accepted in simple terms, for the entire construction is a commentary on invented "realism" in art. Hence the reference to illusionistic classical statues. Art and illusion are a meeting of coincidences.

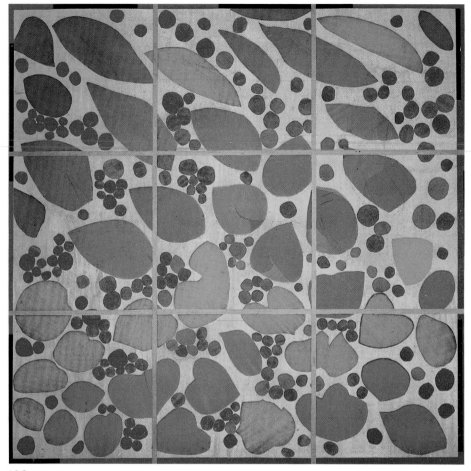

135.

135.
Henri Matisse (French, 1869-1954)
IVY IN FLOWER
1953
collage
h: 112 in., w: 112 in.
Foundation for the Arts Collection,
gift of the Albert and Mary Lasker Foundation
1963.68.FA

136.
Jean Dubuffet (French, b.1901)
THE REVELER
1964
oil on canvas
h: 76 3/4 in., w: 51 1/4 in.
Gift of Mr. and Mrs. James H. Clark
1966.14

In the last years of his life Henri Matisse was too crippled to paint. He began to work with gouache-coated papers, cutting out shapes and having them assembled into large collages. These late paper works have the splendid, clear color sense and feeling of pleasure in life, which may be found in Matisse's work throughout his career. One of the most untroubled of modern artists, Matisse always derived pleasure in the art of making, which is apparent in the masterly ease and ample colorism of the collages made when he was old and dying. *Ivy in Flower,* a design for a stained glass window, superimposes a grid pattern on the cut out shapes. Far from hampering the radiant gaiety of the flowers and ivy leaves, the lines give the work a formal coherence. In this summation of his art, it is easy to see how Mediterranean — how classical in the deepest sense — Matisse was.

In Surrealism, art and literature were closely interwoven, especially in France, where the cultural milieu often produced highly articulate artists. After World War II, Jean Dubuffet, an idiosyncratic writer, painter and polemicist, carried the irrationalism of Surrealism and Dada into a new dimension. While Matisse was glorifying his old age with epic paper collages, Dubuffet was making art that appeared primitive, paradoxical, absurd and extremely witty. He used the mud daubs and graffiti of the modern city in marvelous ways. Almost any shape or material was grist for Dubuffet's iconoclastic mill. In *The Reveler* the human figure is seen as a cheerful and probably drunken jigsaw puzzle; a child's game or scribble becomes sophisticated art. *The Reveler* also seems free and joyous; in his own way Dubuffet expresses as much *joie de vivre* as Matisse.

136.

137.

137.
Rufino Tamayo (Mexican, b.1899)
MAN
1953
vinyl with pigment on masonite
h: 216 in., w: 126 in.
Dallas Art Association Commission,
Neiman-Marcus Company Exposition Funds
1953.22

The reverberations of European modernism were felt everywhere. In Mexico a generation of socially-conscious artists produced monumental art, which adapted abstract forms to a native feel for intense color and sculptural form. Rufino Tamayo's *Man* is a cosmic vision, filled with passionate humanism, which may be compared with Popova's *Painterly Architectonics,* with its revolutionary dynamism. A geometric figure of mankind struggles upwards towards an outburst of comets and stars. The mural painting presents a strong contrast between the dark earth, entangling and hampering the figure, and the radiant blue heaven toward which it strives. The great wedge-shaped thrust of the central image suggests tormented mankind climbing from an open grave up to eternity.

Sculpture

In sculpture, as in painting, 20th century art in France proceeded in an evolutionary way, which was both innovative, since Paris was the center of modern art movements in Europe, and also sensitive to the classical traditions of French art. Between 1910 and the 1920s, a radical development in sculpture occurred all over Europe, but Paris, with the experiments of Cubist art, remained a seminal influence, looked to by artists as far apart as Russia and Spain.

138.

138.
Aristide Maillol (French, 1861-1944)
FLORA
1911
bronze
h: 65 in., w: 19 in., d: 13 1/2 in.
Gift of Mr. and Mrs. Eugene McDermott
1960.70

Like Matisse, Aristide Maillol was a fundamentally Mediterranean and classical artist, absorbed in the sensuous rhythms of the female nude. His works have simplified volumetric forms, and, in some pieces, a dramatic relationship with surrounding space, but they are as much akin to Greco-Roman art as to French modernism. Maillol endeavored to find solid and stable forms, which would recreate in the 20th century the mythic power of antique sculpture. *Flora* is a handsome French peasant girl, turned into a columnar Roman goddess of grace and dignity.

139.
Constantin Brancusi (French, born Rumania, 1876-1957)
BEGINNING OF THE WORLD
c.1920
marble, polished metal disk, stone pedestal
h: 29 5/8 in. (with disc and pedestal), l: 11 3/8 in. (marble)
Foundation for the Arts Collection,
gift of Mr. and Mrs. James H. Clark
1977.51.FA

A similar archetypal imagery is represented by Constantin Brancusi's *Beginning of the World.* Brancusi was an expatriate Rumanian, who settled in Paris in 1904. His sculptures are among the great formative forces in 20th century abstraction. A lover of his materials, Brancusi patiently turned wood, stone and metal into severe, yet evocative, shapes. Often the same idea, such as a bird, fish or woman's head, would be rendered in different media, changing the effect and meaning of the work.

Beginning of the World indicates why Brancusi cannot be called a Cubist, or, indeed, a participant in any particular movement. His abstract forms are radically individual. They also have a ritual element, due to the seriousness of Brancusi's concerns and personality. *Beginning of the World* is just that: the stone cross (symbolic in many cultures), the world disc of metal, and the shining marble egg, which is the source of life. The sublime balance of these parts recalls a universal Genesis; a cosmic mystery is represented with perfect simplicity.

139.

140.
Jacques Lipschitz (French, 1891-1973)
THE BATHER
1923-25
bronze
h: 78 1/8 in., w: 31 1/8 in., d: 27 3/4 in.
Gift of Mr. and Mrs. Algur H. Meadows
and the Meadows Foundation, Incorporated
1967.20

A sculpture much more closely related to Cubism is
Jacques Lipschitz' monumental bronze *Bather*. A massive figure, recognizably human, but primarily abstract
in form, is seen from several angles, which are then
recombined into a unified image. The work has a
very powerful presence, comparable to Léger's *Three
Women and Still Life,* also originating in the 1920s.
In technology, however, Lipschitz utilized traditional
bronze casting methods, as had Maillol, whereas
Brancusi's handmade sculptures were as unusual in
method as in form.

140.

137

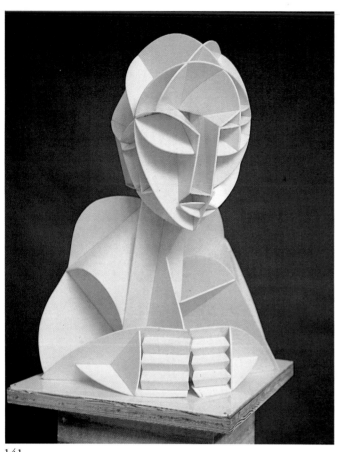

141.

141.
Naum Gabo (American, born Russia, 1890-1977)
CONSTRUCTED HEAD NO. 2
1916, reconstructed c.1923-24
celluloid
h: 17 in., w: 12 1/4 in., d: 12 1/4 in.
The Edward S. Marcus Memorial Fund
1981.35

The distant reaches of Europe often responded as dynamically to the first stages of modern art as did France itself. Kandinsky in Germany, Mondrian in Holland, de Chirico in Italy and Miró in Spain were independent initiators of abstraction or Surrealism, though they were stimulated by ideas coming from Paris. This was especially true in Russia, where the impact of early modern art, in particular Cubism and Futurism, had an effect on the artistic intelligentsia comparable to the revolutionary political situation of the Russian state. The years between 1916 and the early 1920s were ones of great creative enthusiasm among Russian artists. To adapt contemporary abstraction to Russian needs was to assist in the creation of a new society. The bleak realities of Russian authoritarianism soon closed down upon this energetic artistic output, but while it existed it was very innovative.

Naum Gabo began his experimental *Constructed Head #2* during World War I. It is an extraordinary work, which converts a human torso into an analytical structure of open planes, penetrated by light, and so dematerialized. Despite the lightness of the honeycomb effect, the figure has a dense gravity and brooding power. The original sculpture was made of iron; the Museum's version was executed by Gabo in celluloid in the 1920s. Adventurous form was matched by modern material.

142.

143.

142.
Jean Arp (French, 1887-1966)
SCULPTURE CLASSIQUE
1960
bronze
h: 50 in. (with base), w: 8 3/4 in., d: 8 in.
Foundation for the Arts Collection,
given in memory of Mary Seeger O'Boyle
by her family and friends
1966.13.FA

143.
Alberto Giacometti (Swiss, 1901-1966)
THREE MEN WALKING
1948-49
bronze
h: 29 3/4 in., w: 12 1/2 in., d: 13 1/8 in.
Foundation for the Arts Collection,
gift of Mr. and Mrs. Stanley Marcus
1975.86.FA

The persistent power of classicism in France may be seen in a late work by Jean Arp, who was one of the original Surrealist artists, and a poet, as well as a painter and sculptor. His sculptures, despite their avowed connections with Surrealist dream mechanics, always had an elegance and simplicity of form. After World War II, Arp's suave forms made his sculpture widely admired. *Sculpture Classique* simplifies the female nude into an harmonious ovoid shape. While Arp eliminates all appendages, concentrating on the rhythmic curves admired as far back as Greek art, the work's sleek outlines are subtly voluptuous. *Sculpture Classique* recalls Maillol's *Flora,* in its archetypal presentation of Womankind.

Surrealism had diverse descendents. In his early years, the Swiss artist Alberto Giacometti made distinctive sculptures in a Surrealist mode. After World War II, when Giacometti was living in Paris, he became preoccupied with strange elongations of the human figure, to which he devoted the rest of his life. Understanding of Giacometti's work is clouded by the artist's own Orphic (and conflicting) statements. Visually, a work like *Three Men Walking* represents an ambiguous interplay of form and space. The spindly figures, both strongly linear and texturally modelled, pass each other like phantoms. This sense of disembodied loneliness often haunts the viewer of Giacometti's work, but the artist himself seems to have been concerned with modelling figures on the thin line between the Existentialist's Being and Non-Being. The scale and attenuation of his figures also challenges the viewer's sense of optic experience.

144.
Henry Moore (British, b.1898)
RECLINING MOTHER AND CHILD
1974-76
plaster
h: 51 15/16 in., w: 85 1/8 in., d: 41 1/4 in.
Lent by the Henry Moore Foundation
2.1979

In England, Henry Moore's sculptures have a monumentality lacking in Giacometti's elongated figures, but they share a concern for what is irreducibly human in our troubled world. Moore's art suggests rolling hills, primeval stone effigies, bare bones and mythic family groups. His imagery centers on the family, or on mother and child, as the force that continues life.

The genesis Brancusi saw as geometric form, Moore sees as titanic figures, recumbent upon the earth, over whom space flows like a wash of air.

The interaction of space and shape in the Museum's *Reclining Mother and Child* has this plastic vitality. The work also suggests the dynamism of Moore's drawings, as if the figure's outlines were traced upon the surrounding void. Moore's bronze sculptures have the same flowing lines, but in a work like this, which is the original plaster from which bronzes were cast, there is the additional power of seeing forms modelled and impressed by the artist's hands.

144.

145.

145.
Barbara Hepworth (British, 1913-1975)
CONTRAPUNTAL FORMS (MYCENAE)
1965
Carrara marble, teakwood base
h: 37 1/2 in. (with base), w: 51 1/2 in., d: 22 7/8 in.
Gift of Mr. and Mrs. James H. Clark
1971.94

Like Henry Moore, Barbara Hepworth helped to create a traditon of contemporary sculpture in England. She, too, was concerned with the interpenetration of space and form. The gleaming marble halves of *Contrapuntal Forms (Mycenae)* are each pierced by beautifully chiseled holes, adding light and movement to the massive, balanced shapes. This delicate carving is carried out over the whole surface of the marbles, which are modelled in shallow curves. The reference in the title to Greek antiquity is fitting, for the marble group crystallizes wave, mountain and ancient monument into classically pure form.

147.

XII.

American Art: 18th-19th Centuries

The early settlers of North America were hardy, practical people, whose main concerns were taming the wilderness and making a living. They had little time for art; life was too serious for embellishment. The strong Puritan strain in religious life also discouraged image making. Early American art was practical: architectural decoration, furnishings, inn signs, weathervanes. Simple landscapes or rather stiff portraits might be painted by wandering artists, who had little formal training, though much naive skill and charm. An emphasis on utilitarian crafts meant that the first native art was folk art. Wealthier people could import decorative arts for their homes from England.

146.
American
WEATHERVANE: HORSE
c.1840-1860
copper, zinc
h: 19 1/8 in., l: 26 9/16 in.
Foundation for the Arts Collection,
gift of Mr. and Mrs. George V. Charlton
in memory of Edward C. Reed
1977.41.FA

The original living conditions of colonial America followed the frontier westward and the United States remained a largely rural country well into the 19th century. Consequently, folk arts and crafts also remained popular. This handsome zinc and copper weathervane in the shape of a horse was cast in Bridgeport, Massachusetts, in the middle years of the 19th century. Its elegant simplicity is characteristic of American art that was wedded to practicality.

146.

148.

147. *illustration on page 142*
Edward Hicks (American, 1780-1849)
THE PEACEABLE KINGDOM
c.1846-47
oil on canvas
h: 23 7/8 in., w: 31 1/4 in.
The Art Museum League Fund
1973.5

Religious idealism was as characteristic of early America as practical craftsmanship. The Quaker folk artist Edward Hicks painted many versions of his work *The Peaceable Kingdom,* in which the Biblical theme of the lion lying down with the calf, the leopard with the kid and the wolf with the sheepfold is expressed in an Arcadian scene set in Hicks' native Pennsylvania. The animals have a lively, rich decorative appeal, as do the small children, who symbolize innocence. Although there is no true perspective in the painting, the river landscape in the background includes a small scene of William Penn making a peaceful treaty with the Indians, for the land which later became the state of Pennsylvania. Hicks usually included this motif, as it represented historically his dream of natural brotherhood and peace. Hicks' innocent Utopia embodies the vision of hope, freedom and humane progress, in the spirit of which the United States was born.

148.
Gilbert Stuart (American, 1755-1828)
PORTRAIT OF JOHN ASHLEY, ESQUIRE
c.1798
oil on canvas
h: 29 in., w: 24 in.
Munger Fund
1946.37.M

Portraiture was one of the first forms of American art. Like the Dutch merchants of the 17th century, well-to-do Americans valued portraits, because they were symbols of success, as well as records of reality. The demand for portraiture led to an increasing skill and training on the part of the artists who painted them. The first well-known American painters, such as John Singleton Copley and Gilbert Stuart, made their mark in portraiture. While Gilbert Stuart worked extensively in Europe during the 1770s and 1780s, he returned to America, unlike Copley, where he remained until he died in 1828. His main interest in portraiture was a truly American concern for a realistic view of his sitters' faces; he used his conversational charms to awaken their expressions. His portrait of the Philadelphia merchant John Ashley owes its dignified composition to English portraiture, but Mr. Ashley (as well as his wife, whose portrait forms a companion piece to this work) is shown as a solid United States citizen, earnest, educated and prosperous. Stuart wished to show the middle-aged Ashley as well-off, but not pretentious: the best sort of member of the new republic. Stuart's skill is apparent in Mr. Ashley's clear, calm, penetrating gaze and carefully rendered facial forms; he used a similar manner in his celebrated portraits of George Washington.

149.
Frederic Edwin Church (American, 1826-1900)
THE ICEBERGS
1861
oil on canvas
h: 64 1/2 in., w: 112 3/8 in.
Anonymous gift
1979.28

Also as in earlier Dutch art, landscape painting became one of the most important forms of 19th century American art. The Protestant taboo on religious art meant that a great deal of religious feeling went into poetry or paintings about nature. From the works of the Hudson River School onwards, American representations of nature were heavily weighted with emotional meaning. The hand of God lay across the American landscape, waiting to be revealed by the artist's inspired vision.

Frederic Church was one of the most important of these romantic and visionary painters. A pupil of Thomas Cole, who created ambitious, often allegorical landscapes, Church travelled extensively to exotic places like South America, where he could find natural landscapes filled with a sense of the Sublime. The large oil paintings which he worked up from his traveller's sketches were often exhibited for a fee. The *Icebergs* was such a showpiece. Church spent considerable time actually observing icebergs from a ship in the northern Atlantic Ocean and making many of his impressive oil sketches. Later he created his great set-piece, which appears like a window on another world. Despite the meticulous realism in the details, the effect of the painting is grand and romantic in the extreme. Actual nature is transformed into a beautiful, threatening, non-human power, whose destructive force is represented by the broken mast in the foreground. This, the only human element in the work, is a memento of Sir John Franklin's lost arctic expediton. The eerie, translucent blues and greens and golden-whites are icily gorgeous, a Fata Morgana luring men to destruction in the sun-lit frozen wastes.

149.

150.

150.
Albert Bierstadt (American, 1830-1902)
THE MATTERHORN
date unknown
oil on paper mounted on canvas
h: 21 7/8 in., w: 29 7/8 in.
Bequest of Lydia Hartman Bartholow
1971.72

151.
Alfred Thompson Bricher (American, 1837-1908)
TIME AND TIDE
c.1873
oil on canvas
h: 25 1/4 in., w: 50 in.
Foundation for the Arts Collection,
gift of Mr. and Mrs. Frederick M. Mayer
1976.40.FA

Such grandiose landscape paintings had a large audience and were extremely lucrative. Albert Bierstadt made his reputation painting western American scenes with theatrical scope and dynamism. He also painted European landscapes, like this view of the Matterhorn in the Swiss Alps. Bierstadt had observed such scenes while travelling through Europe in the late 1860s. The painting has his customary, carefully rendered details of grass, flowers and rock in the foreground, while behind, the jagged white tooth of the mountain rises abruptly from the pastoral meadows. The scene is romantic, but lacking in Church's visionary poetics.

While Bierstadt's type of broadly painted landscape was popular, other painters created a peculiarly American kind of scene, notable for an extraordinary intensity of light. This style, now often called Luminism, contrives to suggest divine immanence in nature, not by the heroic scale of Church and Bierstadt, but by a radiance that seems to emanate from the forms of the painting. Alfred Bricher's *Time and Tide* (which "wait for no man") has a very sharp, almost blinding clarity, as though the seacoast belongs to a supernatural world.

151.

152.

152.
George Inness (American, 1825-1894)
VIEW OF ROME FROM TIVOLI
1872
oil on canvas
h: 29 7/8 in., w: 45 in.
Foundation for the Arts Collection,
gift of Mrs. John B. O'Hara
in memory of Robert B. O'Hara
1974.14.FA

George Inness made a far more personal and subtle attempt to get beneath the surface of nature and express its spirit. Like many 19th century American artists, he had travelled and studied in Europe, where he learned much about painting out of doors from the artists of the French Barbizon School. Inness, however, remained an American idealist and his softly rendered landscape, *A View of Rome From Tivoli,* has an American sense for the magic of the past, as well as a personal kind of brushwork. The work is luminous with Inness' romantic view of nature. Inness never liked French Impressionism; he continued to explore his own ways of combining the real and the visionary into aerial harmonies.

153.
Thomas Moran (American, b.England, 1837-1926)
AN INDIAN PARADISE, (GREEN RIVER, WYOMING)
1911
oil on canvas
h: 30 in., w: 40 in.
Munger Fund
1950.50.M

The inherent grandeur of western American landscapes was a ready subject for paintings which aimed at spectacular effects, but one that presented problems in representation. As New England writers and painters had complained earlier in the century, America had no visible history to enrich its local scenes. In addition to this lack of human experience to make the West rich in associations, the harsh colors and forms of western sandstones or granites, and the blazing western sunlight pouring down on semi-desert terrain, were very different from the soft green tones of eastern America. Thomas Moran spent most of his career trying to find ways to express the stark splendor of the West in paint. A later work of his, *An Indian Paradise: Green River, Wyoming,* shows one of his solutions. Bleached red and white sandstone is framed by a thin circle of grey-green trees; the colors of the cliff are reflected both in the lake below and in the luminescent sky above. The color harmonies Moran has wrested from the harsh land are matched by the emotional tone of the painting. It is a dream, not reality, for the human figures in the scene are Indians, riding in their natural paradise, which had long since vanished before the course of westward settlement and war.

153.

154.

155.

154.
William Michael Harnett (American, 1848-1892)
MUNICH STILL LIFE
1882
oil on canvas
h: 24 5/8 in., w: 30 1/4 in.
Dallas Art Association purchase
1953.66

The struggle between real and ideal remained present in American art, because Americans were committed to practicality and business, but they also had strong romantic values. Some artists, like William Harnett, devoted considerable technical skill to fool-the-eye paintings, where the objects have such illusionistic clarity as to seem almost surreal. This is not intended ironically, for Harnett and his patrons positively delighted in the smooth art that could render the limp feel of folded newspaper and the fibrous hair of turnip root. American fascination with the thing-in-itself could hardly go further.

156.

155.
John Frederick Peto (American, 1854-1907)
FISH HOUSE DOOR
1905
oil on canvas
h: 30 in., w: 22 in.
Dallas Art Association purchase
1953.17

156.
William T. Ranney (American, 1813-1857)
VETERANS OF 1776 RETURNING FROM THE WAR
1848
oil on canvas
h: 34 1/8 in., w: 48 1/8 in.
The Art Museum League Fund,
Special Contributors, and General Acquisitions Fund
1981.40

Harnett's illusionism was so popular that he had several followers, including John F. Peto, whose *Fish House Door* has a flatter quality than Harnett's richly modelled still life. Peto's painting, with its strange collage of objects and cool colors, has an odd, accidental resemblance to Cubist art. Again, there is no consciousness of the implications of this extreme realism; the lantern and other objects exist absolutely for their own sake, and so have an hallucinatory effect.

An extension of the American taste for simulated reality was the genre scene. Vignettes of ordinary life were painted with detailed realism. Fine artists like George Caleb Bingham, William Sidney Mount or Eastman Johnson could make these scenes genuinely representative of the spirit of American experience. Sometimes, genre scenes were historical, as in William Ranney's *Veterans of 1776 Returning from the War,* but here, too, the figures are represented veristically. With the verve characteristic of genre painters, and an unusually bright pastel range of colors, Ranney dramatizes the freedom and sense of release felt by American volunteer soldiers after the War of Independence.

157.

157.
Thomas Eakins (American, 1844-1916)
PORTRAIT OF MISS GERTRUDE MURRAY
1895
oil on canvas
h: 24 in., w: 20 1/4 in.
Foundation for the Arts Collection,
gift of Mr. and Mrs. George V. Charlton,
Mr. and Mrs. James B. Francis,
Mr. and Mrs. Jake L. Hamon,
and The Jonsson Foundation
1975.1.FA

In the prosperous America of the Gilded Age following the Civil War, artists often felt estranged from the
world around them. "Realism" in art might mean salea-
ble work in one guise and a shock to conventional
taste in another. Thomas Eakins' efforts to paint realistically in the Philadelphia of his time met with little
success. His quiet realism was unappreciated by col-
lectors and he was forced to resign from the Pennsylvania Academy of Fine Arts because he encouraged
drawing from the nude. Isolated from all but his family,
students and a few friends, Eakins continued to paint
life as he saw it; he is now recognized as one of
America's greatest artists. His *Portrait of Miss Gertrude Murray*, like many of his works, projects upon
the woman's features his own sympathetic awareness
of loss and alienation. The painting is a stark contrast
to Manet's *Isabelle Lemonnier* or Morisot's *Lady with
a Muff*. Their happy, heedless vitality is replaced by a
sensitive, inward self-consciousness. Miss Murray could
be the unhappy heroine of Henry James' *Portrait of
a Lady*, whose intelligent sensibility is her undoing.

158.
Winslow Homer (American, 1836-1910)
CASTING IN THE FALLS
1889
watercolor on paper
h: 13 15/16 in., w: 19 15/16 in.
Dallas Art Association purchase
1961.11

Winslow Homer also worked in increasing isolation from commercial America. During the first part of his life he had been, variously, a magazine illustrator, a Civil War reporter and a genre painter of rural scenes. Visits to France in the 1860s and to England in the early 1880s broadened his experience of art, but also toughened his sense of what he, individually, could do as an artist. From the mid-1880s on he lived almost as a recluse on his property in Maine. Like Church, he travelled widely, sketching wherever he went. In this artistic seclusion he created marvelous watercolors, which carried into a more complex world the intense vision of earlier American landscape painting. He concentrated on bold images of primary force: storms, waterfalls, castaway boats at sea, men at odds with an hostile nature. *Casting in the Falls* has this abrupt, dramatic power. The swirling patches of watercolor are his luminous equivalent of Impressionism's swift method of execution in oils.

158.

159.
John Singer Sargent (American, 1856-1925)
PORTRAIT OF DOROTHY
1900
oil on canvas
h: 24 in., w: 19 3/4 in.
Gift of a local foundation
1982.35

Given the limitations of American cultural life at the end of the 19th century, it was not surprising that a number of artists stayed abroad permanently. Just as American heiresses married European noblemen, or Henry James wrote novels about an international society, painters like James McNeil Whistler, Mary Cas-

satt and John Singer Sargent spent most of their working lives in Europe. Sargent, in particular, made his reputation painting portraits of people in high society. His dazzling technique is immediately apparent in his *Portrait of Dorothy,* painted in 1900, when he was at the height of his skill and reputation. Swift, sure and summary brushwork depicts a lavishly dressed little girl with a determined personality. The brilliant glowing whites of her dress and hat are set off by rich apricot tones. Sargent's great gifts were devoted to representing, often with an hidden irony, the upper classes he saw with only too perceptive an eye.

159.

160.

161.

160.
Mary Cassatt (American, 1844-1926)
SLEEPY BABY
c. 1910
pastel
h: 25 1/2 in., w: 20 1/2 in.
Munger Fund
1952.38.M

161.
Childe Hassam (American, 1859-1935)
DUCK ISLAND
1906
oil on canvas
h: 20 1/2 in., w: 31 1/2 in.
Bequest of Joel T. Howard
1951.41

Mary Cassatt also found it necessary for her creative life to live and work in Europe. A close friend of the Impressionists, particularly Degas, she mastered their free painting methods and shared their interest in subjects from everyday life. Her light, high-key colors and fluid brush strokes are typical of Impressionism. However, Cassatt continued to consider herself an American artist and her favorite theme of mother and child does have an American feel for domesticity. The directness and emotional sensitivity of *Sleepy Baby,* as well as its naturalistic simplicity, may be compared with Sargent's bravura style in *Portrait of Dorothy. Sleepy Baby* is in pastel, a medium Cassatt mastered as fully as Degas did. Pinkish-red strokes of the pastel crayon define the firmly modelled bodies of the mother and baby.

Another artist attracted to Impressionism was Childe Hassam. After spending several years in France during the 1880s, Hassam returned to America and initiated a style of American Impressionism. Even more than Mary Cassatt, he remained attached to solidly modelled, three-dimensional forms, unlike the French Impressionists, who usually painted forms dissolved in a play of light. *Duck Island* is a coastal scene in New England, which Hassam painted out of doors. It recalls Monet's great paintings of the cliffs along the coast of Normandy. Where the rocky cliffs painted by Monet form purple and lavender mists of color, blending into sea and sky, Hassam's coast has a chunky Atlantic solidity beneath the light surface pattern of separate brush strokes. Hassam was interested in the reality of the object; Monet in the reality of light.

163.

XIII.

American Art: Early Modern

The divisive problem faced by American artists, who could only learn the most advanced ideas of art in Europe, but who wished to live in America and express a native experience, continued to exist in the first part of the 20th century. The Armory Show of 1913 did reveal the most up-to-date kind of European modernism to New York audiences, but most American artists of the time were more concerned about coming to terms with the persistent American taste for realism, than in adopting European abstraction. As a result, some of the most individual American artists worked largely independently of Europe. When they used abstraction, it tended to be in a personal — one might almost say a homemade — way.

162.
George Bellows (American, 1882-1925)
EMMA IN A PURPLE DRESS
1920-23
oil on canvas
h: 62 in., w: 50 in.
Dallas Art Association purchase
1956.58

George Bellows had been a follower of Robert Henri and the realistic Ashcan School at the turn of the century. He remained attached to an uncompromising, gritty realism, but his portraits became richer and more interesting in the later years of his life, while his narrative scenes became less imaginative and vivid. Shortly before his death, he finished this portrait of his wife Emma, who thought it was the best version of her he had ever done. It combines a warm, painterly richness in handling with a pungent representation of Emma Bellows' forthright personality. She has the lively physical presence of the prize fighters Bellows loved to paint.

162.

163. *illustration on page 156*
Edward Hopper (American, 1882-1967)
LIGHTHOUSE HILL
1927
oil on canvas
h: 28 1/4 in., w: 39 1/2 in.
Gift of Mr. and Mrs. Maurice Purnell
1958.9

Edward Hopper also belongs to the tradition of American realism, but, like Thomas Eakins, he used observed reality to express inward and psychological meanings. His American landscapes appear empty, or frozen in time; they imply a paralyzing loneliness underlying American life. Houses, gas stations, railroad tracks or untenanted cities stand in ghost-like clarity. Hopper's powerful compositional sense, allied with forms of radical simplicity, only enhance this evocative effect. Many of his scenes occur on Cape Cod near his home in Truro, Massachusetts. *Lighthouse Hill* depicts, with Hopper's inimitable sweep and economy, a lighthouse and the keeper's home, rising above grassy dunes. The white shapes stand in massive isolation, lit by a raking light. Hopper painted this scene many times; the lighthouse tower becomes a haunting image of purity and power.

164.
Gerald Murphy (American, 1888-1964)
WATCH
1925
oil on canvas
h: 78 1/2 in., w: 78 7/8 in.
Gift of the artist
1963.75.FA

Gerald Murphy's small body of paintings are part of an unusual episode in American artistic life of the 1920s. Murphy, a well-to-do expatriate, spent only a short time as a painter, producing works which anticipate the later Pop Art of the 1960s. They are bright, stylized images of objects from everyday life. *Watch* demonstrates Murphy's familiarity with Cubist and Surrealist art, for this is not a picture of the works inside a watch, but rather a synthetic image of the idea "watch", with the sound and movement it implies. It is an American parallel to Léger's interest in the symbolism of machinery.

165.
Alexandre Hogue (American, born 1898)
DROUGHT STRICKEN AREA
1934
oil on canvas
h: 30 in., w: 42 1/4 in.
Dallas Art Association purchase
1945.6

With the coming of the Great Depression, artists, too, fell on hard times. Many of them were employed by the Works Progress Administration; others turned to expressing the folk ways of their native areas. The 1930s was a great period for regional art. The Southwestern artist Alexandre Hogue, in *Dought Stricken Area,* provides a gripping picture of the effect of the dust bowl on the High Plains. Cow, house, well and windmill are all skeletons, waiting for the vulture to attack. Hogue's graphic design, recalling folk art, is typical of the populist style common in the 1930s.

164.

165.

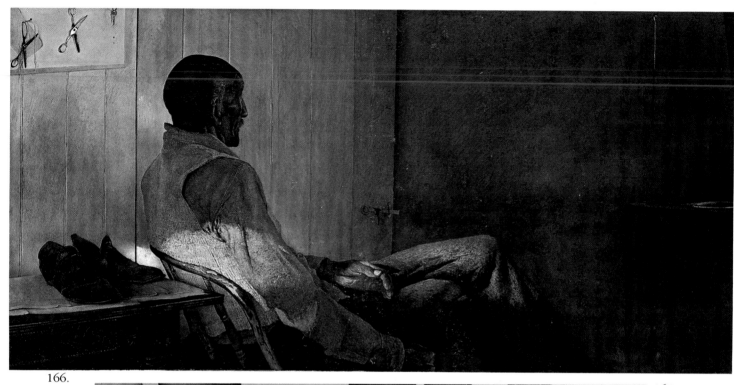

166.

167.

166.
Andrew Wyeth (American, born 1917)
THAT GENTLEMAN
1960
tempera on board
h: 23 1/2 in., w: 47 3/4 in.
Dallas Art Association purchase
1962.27

The 20th century artist closest to the lasting American tradition of poetic realism is Andrew Wyeth, one of a family of artists and illustrators. He is not only meticulous, even compulsive, in his realistic detail, he is also, like Eakins, the painter of lonely, sad and isolated people, caught in the emptiness surrounding successful America. Wyeth's dry, linear style, with its apparitional clarity and subdued range of tones, increases this sense of psychic isolation. The old black man of *That Gentleman* (described by Wyeth as "the finest gentleman I know") has a sad, profound dignity, as he sits quietly in his bare room, enduring his poverty with stoic fortitude.

167.
Georgia O'Keeffe (American, born 1887)
BARE TREE TRUNKS WITH SNOW
1946
oil on canvas
h: 29 1/2 in., w: 39 1/2 in.
Dallas Art Association purchase
1953.1

Hopper's eye for simple and significant shapes is shared by Georgia O'Keeffe, but her semi-abstract imagery has always been based on organic forms. In her later years, spent in the Southwest, O'Keeffe has evolved a personal geometry of rocks, trees and earth, which is strongly impregnated with the spirit of that beautiful desert country. *Bare Tree Trunks with Snow* has a swelling vitality, depicted with strict economy of means. The blues, greys and whites of the winter trees assume a primordial power.

168.
Alexander Calder (American, 1898-1976)
FLOWER
1949
iron, silver, aluminum, paint
h: 102 in., w: 90 in.
Gift of the Dallas Garden Club
1949.13

The American sense of humor had full play in the work of Alexander Calder, who was also one of the few truly innovative American sculptors before World War II. Calder, too, came from a family of artists. His own love for motion and gaiety in art led him to evolve delicately balanced mobiles, which could be stirred by air into constant movement. The Museum's *Flower* lives up to its name, as the airy discs and stars of metal appear to wave gently in the breeze. Calder's generous exuberance and *joie de vivre* led to a vast body of creative sculpture, ranging from miniature figures to giant metal sculptures on the scale of a skyscraper. In all of these works the artist's laughing spirit is visibly at work.

168.

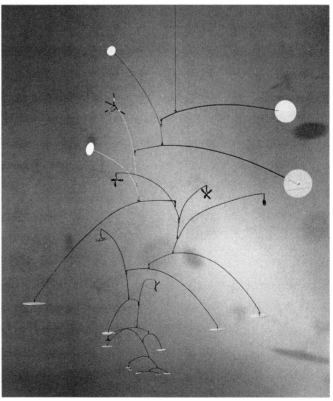

171.

XIV.

American Art: Contemporary Painting

In the years immediately following World War II, the main center of modern art shifted from Europe to America. While there had been distinguished painters in America before this time who had experimented with partial abstraction, art in the United States generally followed where France led. By the 1940s, however, the possibilities opened up by Picasso, Braque, Matisse and Kandinsky no longer seemed so fruitful to American artists. They initiated a series of creative experiments, now loosely called Abstract Expressionism, which were to revolutionize art in the 20th century.

New York was initially the center of this experiment, as it represented culturally a meeting of Old World and New. Expatriate European artists like Mondrian and Léger were working in New York in the 1940s and a number of the leading Abstract Expressionist artists were also foreign-born. Mark Rothko came from Russia, Willem de Kooning from Holland, Hans Hofmann from Germany. New York offered an artistic melting pot where Jackson Pollock, a westerner from Wyoming, could meet other adventurous artists and be exposed to the currently most sophisticated ideas in art, which in turn would stimulate his romantic individualism.

169.
Arshile Gorky (American, b.Armenia, 1904-1948)
Untitled
1943-1948
oil on canvas
h: 54 1/2 in., w: 64 1/2 in.
Dallas Art Association purchase,
Contemporary Arts Council Fund
1965.17

One of the key figures in this development was Arshile Gorky, an American who had come to the United States from Armenia as a boy. A large part of Gorky's career had been devoted to an impassioned discipleship of modern masters like Cézanne, Picasso and Miró. By the 1940s Gorky, having encompassed the European tradition in the way he wished, turned to more intimately personal forms. He re-imagined Surrealist art in ways that expressed his own psychic concerns. His paintings towards the end of his life were ambiguous and secretive, yet eloquent. In the Museum's *Untitled* painting, forms float suggestively, but without context, through a wash of rust, green and pale blue brush strokes.

169.

170.
Jackson Pollock (American, 1912-1956)
CATHEDRAL
1947
enamel and aluminum paint on canvas
h: 71 1/2 in., w: 35 1/16 in.
Gift of Mr. and Mrs. Bernard J. Reis
1950.87

Gorky committed suicide in 1948. At the moment his difficult life was ending, Jackson Pollock was arriving at his distinctive style of painting, in which he dripped colors upon large canvases, laid upon the floor. The brush was replaced by a more dynamic relationship between the artist and his medium: one appropriately called action painting. Gorky had been able to release into visual form his complex emotions; Pollock found a new technique to accomplish this. The term ''Abstract Expressionism'', used to describe this new art, sug-gests its blend of abstract form and personal emotion. Earlier Surrealist art had the same aim, but the work of Pollock had a unique scale and inventiveness, as well as a technique immediately reflecting the artist's control and sensibility, which were quite different from European Surrealism.

Cathedral, one of Pollock's first drip paintings from the late 1940s, demonstrates his masterly control of this new approach to painting. Within the dense interlace of lines, the thickness and texture of each part is orchestrated into an impressive whole. Given the disturbing surges of feeling which Pollock was willing to translate into dripped streams of enamel and aluminum paint, what is most striking about *Cathedral* is its complete coherence of form.

171. *illustration on page 162*
Jackson Pollock (American, 1912-1956)
PORTRAIT AND A DREAM
1953
oil on canvas
h: 58 1/8 in., w: 134 1/4 in.
Gift of Mr. and Mrs. Algur H. Meadows
and the Meadows Foundation, Incorporated
1967.8

In his late and dramatic, self-reflective work, *Portrait and a Dream,* Pollock applies the same mastery to a more overtly Jungian theme. Pollock had spent a considerable time in Jungian analysis, which perhaps led him to objectify his feelings about himself in this striking formal image. One half of the painting is a pure black and white abstraction, a tangle of feeling reduced to controlled form. The colored half is a disembodied image of a human face. The artist's psyche and self, both part of his creativity, face each other in dramatic conjunction.

172.
Mark Rothko (American, b.Russia, 1903-1970)
Untitled
1952
oil on canvas
h: 97 1/2 in., w: 62 1/2 in.
Gift of the Meadows Foundation, Incorporated
1981.133

Like Gorky, Mark Rothko was a European expatriate, whose art expressed both alienation and a search for some meaning that might transcend it. Gorky had adapted European masters; Pollock had been a student of the regional artist Thomas Hart Benton; and Rothko was influenced by Surrealism. All three of these artists had gone beyond their beginnings to a unique, personal style. In Rothko's case, he began to make large paintings, which juxtaposed soft-edged rectangles painted in glowing colors. Until his death in 1970, he painted ever more profound variations on this theme, which expressed his mystical sense of some higher, elusive reality. Color, in a Rothko painting, is like a dimension of the mind or an inner poetic truth.

172.

173.

173.
Franz Kline (American, 1910-1962)
SLATE CROSS
1961
oil on canvas
h: 111 1/4 in., w: 79 in.
Gift of Mr. and Mrs. Algur H. Meadows
and the Meadows Foundation, Incorporated
1968.18

The Abstract Expressionists were never really a school and their art is as varied as their personalities. What they had in common was the excitement of finding a visual voice for America. In the large scale of their works, the heroic ambition of their ideas, and their personal romanticism, they are natural descendants of the 19th century American landscape painters, like Cole, Church, Bierstadt and Moran, who were also trying to join personal passion and vision with the vast scale of America.

Franz Kline's angular black and white paintings have no obvious references to reality, yet they clearly imply the forms of the city: the great bridges, skyscrapers and construction grids of New York. At the same time, they echo the effect of Japanese ink painting, in their bold sweeps of black paint and in brilliant contrasts between form and emptiness, black stroke and white space.

174.

174.
Clyfford Still (American, 1904-1980)
Untitled
1964
oil on canvas
h: 92 in., w: 68 3/4 in.
Gift of the Meadows Foundation, Incorporated
1981.136

175.
Sam Francis (American, b.1923)
EMBLEM
1959
oil on canvas
h: 92 1/2 in., w: 155 3/4 in.
Gift of the Meadows Foundation, Incorporated
1981.117

Where Kline's *Slate Cross* is a vibrant vertical construction, Clyfford Still's work is a complex interplay of jagged red and black shapes, with no marked orientation. Still is austere: if there is emotion in this work, it is much less obvious than with Pollock or Rothko. This is play with paint and painting, to discover its ultimate possibilities, especially the capacity to suggest deep space behind flatly painted forms. Still's distinctive angular, interlocking forms, generally depicted in a few starkly contrasted colors, have a powerful dramatic impact, but one that is formal, rather than emotional. It is the large scale and thick, painterly textures of a work like this, which link Still with Abstract Expressionism.

Although Sam Francis originated in California and has worked both in Europe and on the West Coast, his work is related to the New York School of Abstract Expressionists. His dripped and stained painting technique is indebted to Jackson Pollock, while his areas of brilliant color recall Still. Color has always been Francis' forte. The contrasting halves of *Emblem* present a dynamic balance of primary colors, whose jigsaw shapes suggest an imaginary geography. Unlike Pollock's more uniform web of lines, this work ranges from broad patches of pure color to the thinnest of dripped or dribbled lines.

176.
Robert Motherwell (American, b.1915)
ELEGY TO THE SPANISH REPUBLIC 108
(THE BARCELONA ELEGY)
1966
oil and acrylic on canvas
h: 84 in., w: 147 in.
The Art Museum League Fund
1967.7

Robert Motherwell, throughout his career, has had closer ties to the classics of European modernism than the other Abstract Expressionists. An intellectual and theorist on art, he creates art that has a conscious elegance quite different from the raw power of Pollock, Still or Kline. Yet his paintings are also full of emotional meaning. In his ongoing series of works on the theme of the Spanish Civil War, Motherwell created monumental forms — massive black vertical shapes against a lighter background — which are forceful images of life and death, as well as being evocative of the Spanish landscape.

Elegy to the Spanish Republic, #108 suggests a grim monolith from Mediterranean prehistory or the sinister black body of a bull, shadowing the clear blue and white of Mediterranean sunlight. Motherwell's masterly control of a work massive in scale and effect is a classic example of the new visual realm American artists created in the post-war period.

177.
Mark Tobey (American, 1890-1976)
ECHOES OF BROADWAY
1964
tempera on paper
h: 52 1/4 in., w: 25 1/2 in.
Gift of the artist.
1967.18

While the large work and the dynamic painting methods of the Abstract Expressionists revolutionized American art during the 1950s, a number of important artists pursued different, very personal ends. In the Pacific Northwest, Mark Tobey was attracted both to oriental religions and to Japanese writing and ink painting. He evolved an intricate style of tempera painting, which seemed to be the record of some unknown, poetic language. Whorls and tracery of white lines form a mysterious, suggestive pattern. *Echoes of Broadway* is a meditation, where Pollock's *Cathedral* is a forceful assertion.

177.

178.
Morris Louis (American, 1912-1962)
BROAD TURNING
1958
acrylic on canvas
h: 90 in., w: 150 in.
Gift of Mr. and Mrs. Algur H. Meadows
and the Meadows Foundation, Incorporated
1971.68

Morris Louis, working alone in Washington D.C. during the 1950s, arrived at a type of painting related to Abstract Expressionism in scale and experimental character, but without its emotional fireworks. His art is concerned with color for its own sake, freed from personal reference. Acrylic paints were stained into unprimed canvas, producing webs and flows of softly modulated tones. Louis' paintings are sensuous to a marked degree, and their serene character can be seen as contrasting strongly with action painting. His painterly art was to influence a generation of Color Field artists.

179.
Jim Dine (American, b.1935)
SELF-PORTRAIT NEXT TO A COLORED WINDOW
1964
charcoal on canvas; oil on glass and wood
h: 71 7/8 in., w: 99 1/2 in.
Dallas Art Association purchase,
Contemporary Arts Council Fund
1965.1

The loneliness and isolation so typical of the artist in modern America is the subject matter of Jim Dine's *Self-Portrait Next to a Colored Window.* It is a gently ironic self-image: the artist appears as a headless monochromatic charcoal figure in a bathrobe, silhouetted against a grid pattern. The right half of the work includes the same grid, filled with brightly colored glass squares, which represents the window display of his father's paint store. The childhood memory is more alive and vital than the anonymous figure of the artist. Much of Dine's work involves a subtle, self-conscious play with the nature of art and the artist's relation to his medium.

178.

179.

180.

180.
Jasper Johns (American, b.1930)
DEVICE
1961-62
oil on canvas with wood
h: 72 in., w: 48 1/8 in., d: 2 3/4 in.
Gift of the Art Museum League,
Mrs. and Mrs. George V. Charlton,
Mr. and Mrs. James B. Francis,
Dr. and Mrs. Ralph Greenlee, Jr.,
Mr.and Mrs. James H.W. Jacks,
Mr. and Mrs. Irvin L. Levy,
Mrs. John W. O'Boyle, and Dr. Joanne Stroud
in honor of Mrs. Eugene McDermott
1976.1

A more dramatic embodiment of this theme is Jasper Johns' *Device*. During the 1950s and 1960s Johns created a series of modern icons — maps, numbers, the American flag — which were notable for their vibrant colored textures. Elements of ordinary life were suddenly given an improbable aesthetic richness. Pop artists also used this kind of subject matter, but Johns' work has always been remarkable for a distinguished, dispassionate irony. In *Device,* the element of ironic play is the subject of the painting, which includes segments of circles and actual canvas stretchers, as well as the word DEVICE. The forms suggest geometry, construction, and the Renaissance idea of the artist as a master craftsman, while the wealth of blue and red-orange paint, thick and palpable to the touch, pours over the whole surface of the painting with an independent life of its own.

181.

181.
Richard Lindner (American, b.Germany, 1901-1978)
ROCK-ROCK
1966
oil on canvas
h: 70 in., w: 60 in.
Gift of Mr. and Mrs. James H. Clark
1968.14

The use of images from everyday life became a full-scale movement, Pop Art, in the 1960s. Elements of the real world, which had been ignored in Abstract Expressionism, reappeared, but exaggerated and simplified. Richard Lindner converted sleazy figures from the modern city into hieratic figures of strident power. In *Rock-Rock,* a rock musician becomes one image with his electric guitar. It is a work full of garish eroticism. The bands of bright color pulsate at high volume, like the musician's piercing sound. With a single powerful figure, Lindner sums up a whole era of American culture.

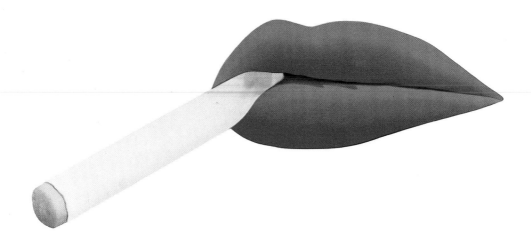

182.

182.
Tom Wesselmann (American, b.1931)
MOUTH #11
1967
oil on canvas
h: 67 1/2 in., w: 154 in.
Foundation for the Arts Collection,
gift of Mr. and Mrs. Edward S. Marcus Foundation
1968.7.FA

Pop Art's relation to commercial art is clear in Tom Wesselmann's *Mouth #11,* a billboard-size shaped canvas work of a woman's mouth with a cigarette. Like the billboard, *Mouth's* giant image has visual impact from a considerable distance, but the painting offers a sardonic view of American sensuality and the advertising which panders to it.

183.
James Rosenquist (American, b.1933)
PAPER CLIP
1973
oil and acrylic on canvas
h: 102 in., w: 223 1/2 in.
Gift of The 500, Inc.,
Mrs. Elizabeth B. Blake,
Mr. and Mrs. James H.W. Jacks,
Mr. and Mrs. Robert M. Meltzer,
Mr. Joshua Muss, Mrs. John W. O'Boyle,
Mrs. R.T. Shalom, and Dr. Joanne Stroud
in honor of Robert M. Murdock
1978.28

Few modern American artists feel at home in a mass civilization. Their visions of it range from mild criticism to political castigation. James Rosenquist's *Paper Clip* is an example of a Pop Art painting with strongly implied social commentary. Even more than *Mouth #11, Paper Clip* approximates to a billboard in its great size and clean, sharply defined shapes, but the

images are elements of ordinary life — ticker tape, paper clips, Mobil Oil Company's Flying Red Horse — taken out of context, magnified, and given allegorical power. It is an epic view of industrial society, where people live in the power of forces at once trivial and irresistible.

184.
Al Held (American, b.1928)
D-C
1979
acrylic on canvas
h: 96 in., w: 168 in.
Matching grants from the National Endowment for the Arts
and The 500, Inc., and General Acquisitions Fund
1980.37

The scale and hard-edged clarity of Rosenquist's work is also found in this more purely abstract painting by Al Held. A vast complexity of geometric forms, which denies spatial or rational logic, makes an intricate network of square, diagonal and paraboloid shapes. This dazzling non-rational maze is both flat and three-dimensional at the same time. Held plays with perspective forms in a manner reminiscent of Piranesi or M.C. Escher, creating a mad mathematics of Einsteinian space.

The hot colors seem to race backward and forward along the diagonals of the painting, like flashes of electronic light. *D-C* is an ambitious work, considerably advanced beyond Held's previous black and white images, and it appears to suggest the ambiguous, unreachable structure of the physical universe.

83.

84.

185.

185.
Richard Diebenkorn (American, b.1922)
OCEAN PARK NO. 29
1970
oil on canvas
h: 100 in., w: 81 in.
Gift of the Meadows Foundation Incorporated
1981.106

186.
William T. Wiley (American, b.1937)
PAINTING FOR RAIN
1976
acrylic and charcoal on canvas
h: 93 in., w: 183 in.
Foundation for the Arts Collection,
anonymous gift in memory of Edward S. Marcus
1976.72.FA.

The frequency with which contemporary artists create works in series reflects the artists' great concern for formal technique. Variations on a theme make possible an in-depth exploration of a particular style, subject or method. Since moving to Santa Monica in 1967, the California artist Richard Diebenkorn has painted a series of works called *Ocean Park,* after the area near his studio. These are large, vertical paintings, organized by linear forms which gently articulate the dense layers of paint on the canvas. They are open and softly glowing in color, with gentle blues and golds and pinkish-lavenders, which incarnate the magic sunlight of Los Angeles. Diebenkorn has always considered himself to be a landscape painter, and his paintings, though appearing to be pure abstractions, have evocative, poetic memories of people, buildings and seascapes washed by the California sun.

Art in California often seems more humanistically oriented than art in New York. William Wiley's painting is a wonderfully individualistic blend of abstract form, visual and verbal puns, personal references, and metaphysical imagery. The California scene rendered by Diebenkorn as luminous abstraction is recreated by Wiley as a series of colorful puzzle pictures. Realistic detail, even written phrases, are absorbed into a dense overall pattern. He is a landscape painter of the California psyche. *Painting For Rain* (actually painted during an extended period of drought) is a good example of his homemade magic iconography. The black and white surveyor's rod, which appears in other Wiley paintings as a magician's staff, here takes the form of a spiral, or rain charm, hovering over the dry California countryside.

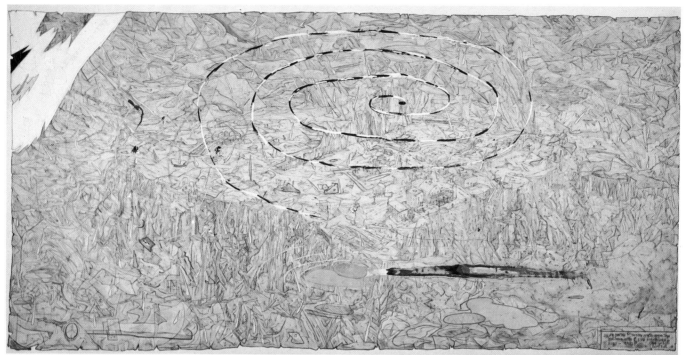

186.

187.

187.
Sylvia Mangold (American, b.1938)
SCHUNNEMUNK MOUNTAIN
1979
oil on canvas
h: 59 15/16 in., w: 80 1/8 in.
General Acquisitions Fund
and a gift from The 500, Inc.
1980.7

Yet another example of an artist playing with the elements of art is Sylvia Mangold's *Schunnemunk Mountain,* in which a night landscape scene is framed by larger painted rectangles and fool-the-eye masking tape. The country scene visible from the artist's New York State studio is not painted for its own sake, but as part of a commentary on the nature of construction in art. It raises questions about illusionism. What is the artist doing when he "represents reality"? What is the value of a landscape painting today? What is the point to the technical tricks of perspective? There are no answers to these questions; instead, the artist presents an interchange between the poetic, dark mountain view and the artist's mind at work.

188.

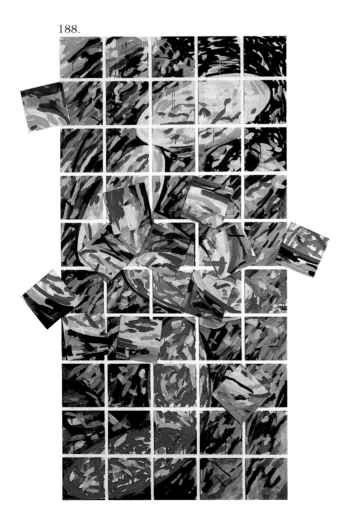

189.

188.
Jennifer Bartlett (American, b.1941)
SAD AND HAPPY TIDAL WAVE
1978
enamel, silkscreen on steel plate (62 plates);
oil an canvas (2 panels)
h: 129 1/2 in., w: 172 in.
Foundation for the Arts Collection,
gift of Susan and Robert K. Hoffman
1979.9.a-c.FA

189.
Richard Shaffer (American b.1947)
PLATFORM WITH STAIRS
1980-81
oil on canvas
h: 111 1/2 in., w: 192 in.
General Acquisitions Fund
and gifts from two anonymous donors
1981.26

In direct contrast to the muted sensibility of *Schunnemunk Mountain* is the exuberant work of Jennifer Bartlett. *Sad and Happy Tidal Wave,* part of her *Swimmer* series, is a diptych. Half of the work is painted canvas, the other half Bartlett's distinctive painted steel tiles. Both halves center on an abstract figure of a swimmer, composed of oval shapes, but there is a strong contrast between the flatter, softer, and more organic version on the canvas, and the brilliant shiny, geometric effect of the tiles. This work, too, presents the artist playing with the characteristics of media.

In recent years illusionistic realism, or the representation of objects with photographic clarity, has been an important element of contemporary art. At first glance, Richard Shaffer's *Platform with Stairs* might seem to belong to this movement, as the scene in his studio is painted with illusionistic precision. The stark quality of the forms in the painting, however, is closer to geometric abstraction, while the meditative intensity of his work is far removed from any fascination for the "thing in itself." His work is a recent example of the American desire to combine the realistic and the visionary.

190.

XV.

American Art: Contemporary Sculpture

A similar development to that in painting occurred in American sculpture after World War II, though without a dynamic explosion comparable to Abstract Expressionism. Before this period, only Calder had really anticipated the formal experiments made by sculptors in the use of new materials and in constructive spatial ideas. New *uses* for sculpture in America have complemented the artists' creativity. The commission of large-scale sculptures for corporate buildings or public spaces has stimulated the invention of works suitable to such sites. Environmental design has extended the idea of sculpture into a modification of the landscape. The line between crafts and sculpture has become less distinct, bringing about an interchange between artists in these fields. Cities whose visual appearance is due to industrial design have suggested the use of industrial materials and factory trained workmen as extensions of the artist's hands. Remote as all these events are from the 19th century *Weathervane* in the shape of a horse, they recall the fact that American art began as the offspring of utilitarian crafts.

190.
David Smith (American, 1906-1965)
CUBI XVII
1963
stainless steel
h: 107 3/4 in., w: 64 3/8 in., d: 38 1/8 in.
The Eugene and Margaret McDermott Fund
1965.32.McD

The unquestioned master of this period in American sculpture is David Smith. Using industrial steel and factory welding techniques, he created a landscape of dynamic metal forms. As a friend of several Abstract Expressionist painters, he shared their revolutionary fervor, but his art rarely tried to express difficult emotions. Instead, its brilliance is classical and humanist, rather than romantic.

Towards the end of his life, Smith created a series of geometric stainless steel constructions, called *Cubi,* of which the Museum's *Cubi XVII* is an example. Human in their frontal stance and balance, and dazzling in their radiance of wire-brushed steel, the *Cubi* sculptures have an effortless realization of mathematical form easily comparable to the Museum's classic Greek statue. Both are Platonic in their ideal purity.

191.

191.
Anthony Caro (British, b.1924)
VEDUGGIO SUN
1972-73
steel, rusted and varnished
h: 100 in., w: 117 in., d: 54 in.
Mr. and Mrs. Edward S. Marcus Fund
1974.13

Smith's untimely death at the age of 59 left no imme-diate American heir to his genius, but a young British sculptor, Anthony Caro, who had worked with Smith, continued his vision in a new way. Working both in America and England, Caro has employed industrial steel I-beams, tubes, sheet metal, steel rollings and mill scraps, to create linear and planar forms project-ing into space. Smith's classic balance is replaced by a more evocative art, with allusions to prehistoric mon-uments or architectural forms. While some Caro works are brilliantly colored, *Veduggio Sun* has the warm patina of rusted metal.

192.
Tony Smith (American, 1912-1980)
WILLY
designed 1962, fabricated 1978
steel
h: 91 1/4 in., w: 224 in., d: 144 in.
Irvin L. and Meryl P. Levy Endowment Fund
and General Acquisitions Fund
1977.72

Monumental metal sculpture is one of the major forms of contemporary American sculpture, as it is in scale with large buildings and reflects the building materials which envelop modern life. The concept of sculpture related to the human form and organic shapes is replaced by the concept of sculpture as machine or construction. The assertive brilliance of skyscrapers and highway interchanges has influenced the nature of sculptural form.

Tony Smith was an artist familiar with architecture as well as sculpture; his work spans both kinds of construction. The uncluttered geometry of a work like *Willy* has the force of an architectural building. Both the form of the dark metal tetrahedron and the space it shapes seem to be bent, effortlessly, by some invisible mechanical force. It is like an excerpt from a building process.

193.
Richard Serra (American, b.1939)
Untitled
1971
steel
h: 96 in., w: 192 in., d: 150 in.
Matching grants from the National Endowment for the Arts and The 500, Inc., in honor of Mr. and Mrs. Leon Rabin
1976.24

The weight and density of Cor-Ten steel is emphasized by Richard Serra's massive pieces, which deliberately suggest a sense of ponderous, even dangerous, balance. The effect is both psychological and physical. Simple as the forms of the Museum's Serra sculpture are, their dramatization of opposing tensions has an ominous power.

194.)
Mark di Suvero (American, b.1933)
AVE
1973
painted steel
h: 478 in., w: 370 in., d: 545 in.
Irvin L. and Meryl P. Levy Endowment Fund
1976.10

A work which was a spectacular complement to the old Museum building and is one of the high points of the outdoor sculptures around the new institution, is Mark di Suvero's *Ave.* Like David Smith, di Suvero is an artist of generous humanist temperament. All of his works have an immediate human appeal, as well as formal elegance and power. *Ave* is a grandiose construction of crimson-painted steel I-beams, with soaring diagonals and aerial thrusts, yet it is designed for children to climb upon. Baroque in its dynamic verve, it is Baroque, too, in being an impressive public sculpture, about which people may walk, play or amuse themselves.

195.
Carl Andre (American, b.1935)
PYRAMID (SQUARE PLAN)
1959(destroyed); 1970(remade)
wood (fir)
h: 68 7/8 in., w: 31 in., d: 31 in.
General Acquisitions Fund
and matching funds from The 500, Inc.
1979.44

Although the present form of this sculpture dates to
1970, its original creation was in 1959. It is a seminal
work, not only in Carl Andre's career, but in the development of contemporary sculpture. It was one of the
first works which Andre made by piling up identical
wooden shapes in a geometric construction, which
had no bonding material. In doing this, he abandoned
the idea of sculpture as a carved or chiseled unity. As
David Smith had used industrial steel, Andre used
readily available standard wood two-by-fours. The fir
wood modules are simply stacked in an interlocking
double pyramid pattern, forming a shape which is
elegant, yet still redolent of Andre's raw materials.
Nor can this be called simply geometric abstraction,
for Andre (who counts Brancusi as one of his ancestors) remains a craftsman, tied to the feel and the
symbolic implications of his medium, about which
he has said, "Wood is the bride of life in death, of
death in life".

196.
Robert Morris (American, b.1931)
Untitled
1965-66
wood, fiberglass, fluorescent tubing
h: 24 in., w: 14 in., dia: 96 in.
General Acquisitions Fund
and matching grant from the National Endowment for the Arts
1974.145

Andre's work in the 1950s and early 1960s had a
wide influence, especially on the artists working in
the Minimalist style, which involved prefabricated
materials and simple geometric forms. Robert Morris'
work in the Museum collection is a deceptively simple doughnut shape, in wood and fiberglass with fluorescent lighting. It exemplifies the chaste reductions
of the Minimalist aesthetic. Form speaks for itself, in
geometric purity; material is subdued and neutral in
color; the artist's sensibility operates in subtle ways,
like the light areas separating the two halves of the
circle.

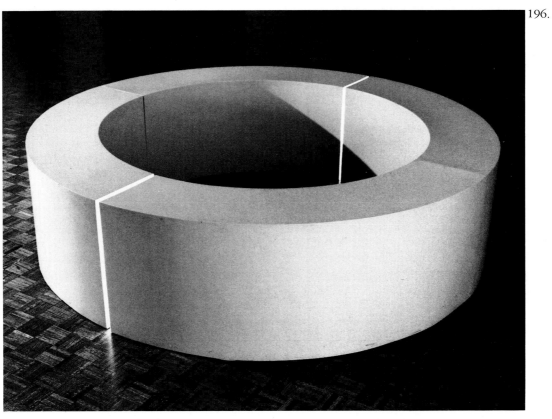

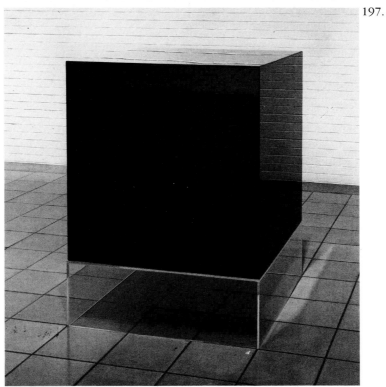

197.
Larry Bell (American, b.1939)
THE CUBE OF THE ICEBERG II
1975
1/2 inch float glass coated with iconel and silicon monoxide
h: 36 in., w: 36 in., d: 36 in.
Anonymous gift in memory of J.O. Lambert, Jr.
1981.44

An equally pristine conception is Larry Bell's *Cube of the Iceberg II*. A West Coast artist now working in Taos, Bell creates geometric forms in coated glass. The dark square of *Cube of the Iceberg II* sits on a clear rectangular base, over which the cube seems to float. The Minimalist attraction to unadorned shapes and man-made materials lies behind the apparent simplicity of Bell's work. The glass panels he uses are factory fabricated to his specifications, not hand-made. Bell's art, however, has a more resonant and mystical feeling than Minimalist art usually does. Glass has the unique quality of being present and not present at the same time, a state Bell continues to explore.

198.
Joel Shapiro (American, b.1941)
Untitled
1975
cast iron
h: 2 5/8 in., w: 4 3/4 in., d: 6 1/4 in.
Matching grants from the National Endowment for the Arts
and The 500, Inc.
1975.83

As Larry Bell has investigated the possibilities of emptiness and spatial negation in glass, Joel Shapiro has experimented with people's experience of size, mass and weight inherent in sculpture. In the Museum's example of Shapiro's work, the openings in the small rectangular form lead, not to space, but to a dark, invisible center. The work simultaneously suggests and denies one's idea of a building. Most of Shapiro's works disorient and stimulate the viewer in this oblique way. They are often startlingly small in size, yet have the apparent weight of much larger sculptures, as if they were dwarf stars, packed with dense gravity.

198.

199.
Alan Saret (American, b.1941)
DEEP FOREST GREEN DISPERSION
1969
painted wire
h: 96 in., w: 36 in.(variable)
Gift of John Weber
1977.71

The wide array of materials available to contemporary sculptors has made possible work in which the form of the art is suggested by its substance. Alan Saret has utilized chicken wire and fencing materials to shape openwork constructions, which distantly recall trees or human figures. The airy green cloud of *Deep Forest Green Dispersion* embodies organic form in an abstract medium, while the homely chicken wire assumes an improbable grace and delicacy.

200.

199.

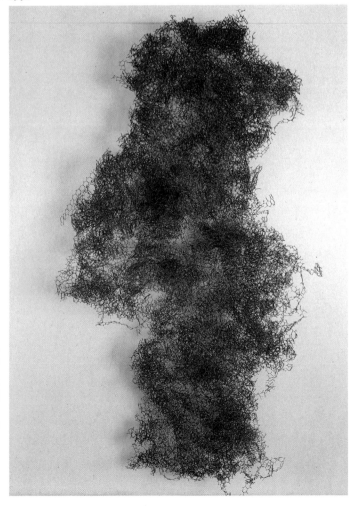

200.
James Surls (American, b.1943)
ONCE I SAW A SPOTTED LADY
WHOSE BELLY WAS ROUND LIKE A BALL
1974
wood, wool
h: 46 3/4 in., w: 27 1/2 in., d: 26 1/2 in.
General Acquisitions Fund
1974.10

The Texas artist James Surls uses wood in a rough-hewn, unfinished and rugged manner. The feel of *tree* is present in his work, as it is in African sculptures. His anthropomorphic forms and psychologically disturbing imagery, often full of a charged sexuality, also recall African art. This piece, which was originally suggested by the sight of a pregnant woman in a supermarket, has Surls' typical spiky, thrusting forms and burnt ornamentation on the trunk of the figure. It is a bold, surreal image of primitive power. Surls grew up in the Texas countryside and now lives on forested land north of Houston; his art retains these rural roots and seems a natural outgrowth of his feeling for trees.

201.
Deborah Butterfield (American, b.1949)
HORSE #6-82
1982
steel, sheet aluminum, wire, tar
h: 76 in., w: 108 in., d: 41 in.
Foundation for the Arts Collection,
Edward S. Marcus Fund
1982.96.FA

Another sculptor with strong ties to the countryside is Deborah Butterfield, an artist working in Montana, whose sculpture is devoted to celebrating horses. These are not real horses, but magic animals, who represent the artist's *alter ego*. Made of scrap metal or odds and ends Butterfield has collected, the full-size horse figures have a blind and brooding power. They do not represent nostalgia for a lost rural past, any more than James Surl's powerful wood sculptures do: the horses are psychic symbols of an animal side to man's nature, which remains valid in the present day.

201.

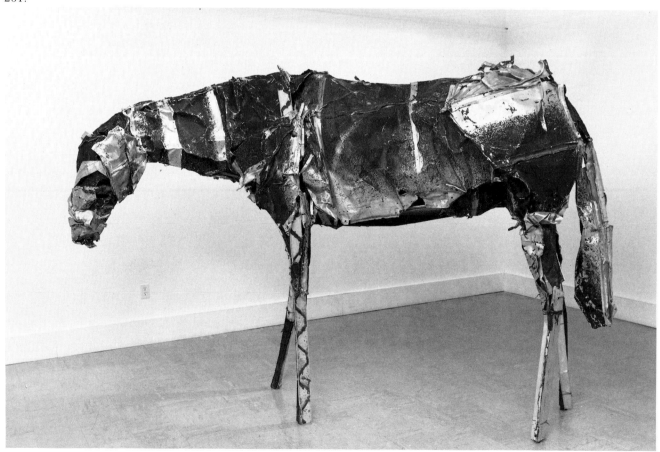

202.

202.
Kenneth Price (American, b.1935)
DE CHIRICO'S BATHHOUSE
1980
ceramic
a: h: 8 1/4 in., w: 8 15/16 in., d: 3 1/16 in.
b: h: 27/32 in., w: 4 3/8 in., d: 2 1/2 in.
Foundation for the Arts Collection, anonymous gift
1981.10.a-b.FA

The contemporary meeting of art and craft is apparent in Kenneth Price's ceramic sculpture. While *De Chirico's Bathhouse* has the small size of utilitarian pottery, and also alludes to actual objects like a cup, it is an independent sculptural form. Where the masterworks of Chinese or Greek ceramics used aesthetic design to heighten the appeal of a practical utensil, Price uses the techniques of ceramics - solid clay shapes and brightly colored glazes — to make a complex object, which deliberately echoes earlier art styles like Constructivism or Surrealism. Small as the piece is, its vibrant colors and angular shapes give it considerable presence. The ironic title, recalling the fantasies of Giorgio de Chirico, underlines the work's ambiguous sources in both art and pottery.

Several important works of contemporary sculpture were commissioned for the new Museum building. Recognizing that sculpture is a strong point of the Dallas Museum of Art's collections, every effort was made to find works which, in scale and importance, would complement the Museum's architecture. This was an opportunity for collaboration between the architect, Edward Larrabee Barnes, and important contemporary artists.

203.)
Claes Oldenburg (American, B.Sweden, 1929)
Study for Stake Hitch, (with figure for scale)
1983
pencil, chalk, watercolor
h: 41 in., w: 27 3/4 in.

STAKE HITCH
1983
painted steel and aluminum, expanded foam and reinforced resin
upper stake: h. 192 in. (approx.)
lower stake: h. 144 in. (approx.)
rope: h. 288 in., dia. 20 in. (approx.)
Commissioned to honor John Dabney Murchison, Sr.
for his arts and civic leadership, and presented
by his Family

One of the most striking of these new commissions is Claes Oldenburg's giant *Stake Hitch,* designed for the barrel vaulted central court of the Contemporary Art galleries. It is similar to such monumental creations of Oldenburg's as the *Lipstick Monument* at Yale University and the *Batcolumn* in Chicago, but differs from them in being placed inside a building. The work is an 18-foot-high painted metal stake, attached to the 40-foot-high roof of the vault by a huge rope. The tip of the stake is installed in the Museum's basement area under the gallery floor. Pop Art on a gigantic scale, *Stake Hitch* dominates even the very large spaces of the vaulted court.

With its suggestions of Texas cowboys and tent stakes, *Stake Hitch* joins other examples of everyday objects, which Oldenburg has magnified to grandiose proportions. Its color, scale and character are in strong contrast with the elegant, refined architecture of the Museum building, and add a dynamic sense of drama to it. Oldenburg's sculptures are unique in their fusion of grandeur and comedy, a combination likely to stimulate Museum visitors who encounter *Stake Hitch* at the heart of the collection of Contemporary art.

204.
Richard Fleischner (American, b.1944)
Plan for Education Courtyard
1982
chalk on diazo print
h: 24 in., w: 29 13/16 in.

Elevation for East Wall of Education Courtyard
1982
chalk on diazo print
h: 24 in., w: 39 13/16 in.

Courtyard for The Dallas Museum of Art
l: 115 ft., w: 115 ft.
Commissioned to honor Minnie and Albert Susman
on the occasion of their 50th anniversary by their children
Robert F. and Anna Marie Susman Shapiro

The size of Oldenburg's sculpture actually makes it part of the architectural experience of the Museum. This is even more true of Richard Fleischner's site-specific work for the Education Courtyard. Fleischner is an artist working in Providence, Rhode Island, whose project, submitted as an entry in an invitational competition by the Museum, was selected to create this space. It was essential that the design would function effectively for Education Department programs and also be visually integrated into the Museum's architecture.

Fleischner's work includes a sculptural square of flowering trees in the center of the courtyard, surrounded by planes and platforms of limestone, upon which art activities and creative dramatic presentations can take place. The scale and detail of the courtyard are adapted to the limestone exterior of the Museum and harmonize gracefully with its lines and detailing. Space, textures and trees form a plastic whole, which is also an enveloping aesthetic experience.

204.

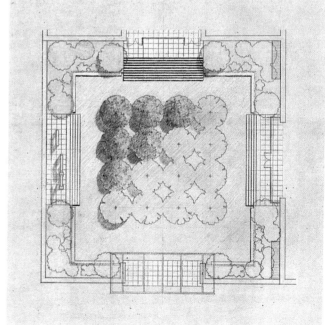

205.
Scott Burton (American, b.1939)
Granite Settee
1983
granite
h: 36 in., w: 65 in., d: 35 in.
National Endowment for the Arts grant
with matching funds from Robert K. Hoffman,
the Roblee Corporation, Laura L. Carpenter,
Nancy M. O'Boyle and an anonymous donor

The inter-relationships between a museum goer's experience and these non-traditional, all-encompassing art works also occurs in Scott Burton's granite settee. Burton's work is concerned with furniture, the forms of which are created in hard materials like granite, which seem antagonistic to the function of furniture. Burton, however, carefully considers the human use of his monumental creations; they are comfortable to sit on, despite their massive appearance and seemingly hard surface.

Granite settee consists of six blocks of granite shaped into irregular geometric forms and placed together with no bonding material. The stark blocks suggest a prehistoric shrine, which is, paradoxically, congenial and usable.

205.

206.)
Ellsworth Kelly (American, b.1923)
Model for Dallas Sculpture
1982
stainless steel
h: 8 3/8 in., w: 14 5/8 in., d: 16 in.

Untitled
1983
stainless steel
h: 120 in., w: 228 in., d: 204 in.
Commission made possible through funds donated by Michael J.
Collins and matching grants from The 500, Inc. and the 1982
Tiffany & Company benefit opening

A commissioned work by Ellsworth Kelly is situated in a commanding central position at one end of the reflecting pool in the Museum's Sculpture Garden. Although Kelly is best known for his two-dimensional, hard-edged paintings with contrasting areas of color, he is equally important as a sculptor. In three-dimensional work, as in his painting, Kelly explores the relationship of edge, plane and color.

The Museum's sculpture seems to be completely abstract, but Kelly often has natural imagery in mind as he makes his sculptures; he has said this form recalls a wounded bird. The piece consists of two stainless steel segments of a circle, which are folded at the top. The frontal opening is 10-feet high, making it possible to walk into the sculpture's space. The delicately balanced curving planes appear lightly positioned on the ground, despite the 18,000 lb. weight of the steel. Visually, they seem poised on the edge of a rocking movement, intimating the ''Rocker'' title Kelly gives to this series of shapes.

XVI.

Prints, Drawings and Photographs

On the first floor of the Museum, in the same quadrant as the art history library and the visual resources laboratory, there is storage, study and display space for the Museum's works on paper. These collections will be available for scholarly study, rather than being placed in inaccessible storage. In addition, there is a large room for changing exhibits of prints, drawings and photographs, either ones drawn from the Museum's collections, or from travelling exhibitions organized elsewhere. One purpose of the new Dallas Museum of Art is to serve as a scholarly resource for the community; this area, with the accompanying textile collection, is intended to implement that concept.

Prints

While the largest number of prints in the collection are contemporary, there also exists a reasonably good survey of historically important printmakers since the Renaissance.

207.
Rembrandt van Rijn (Dutch, 1606-1669)
THE ANGEL APPEARING TO THE SHEPHERDS
1634
etching, engraving and drypoint, 3rd state
h: 10 1/4 in., w: 8 5/8 in. (image)
Gift of Calvin J. Holmes
1963.38

The Angel Appearing to the Shepherds is one of a number of prints by Rembrandt Van Rijn in the collection. This complex print, which combines Baroque splendor in the heavenly vision with homely Dutch realism in the group of shepherds, reveals Rembrandt's mastery of texture, line and chiaroscuro in graphics, as well as oil painting.

208.

209.

208.
William Blake (British, 1757-1827)
BOOK OF JOB, PLATE 2:
WHEN THE ALMIGHTY WAS YET WITH ME
1825
engraving, chine collé, 2nd state
h: 7 7/8 in., w: 6 1/16 in. (image)
Gift of the Junior League of Dallas
1940.1

The English Romantic poet William Blake created prints closely allied to his visionary poetry. In this engraving for the Book of Job, text is as important as illustration, and both are united in Blake's intricate decorative style, where willowy figures, like disembodied wraiths of Michelangelo's sculpture, ascend to the throne of God.

209.
Käthe Kollwitz (German, 1867-1945)
IN MEMORY OF KARL LIEBKNECHTS
1919-20
woodcut with black and white brush highlights, 2nd state
h: 13 3/4 in., w: 19 3/4 in. (image);
h: 17 1/2 in., w: 22 3/8 in. (sheet)
Gift of Mrs. A.E. Zonne
1942.109

The emotional power of German Expressionism is seen in a rare woodcut by Käthe Kollwitz, which was retouched with brush highlights by the artist herself. The mourning for Karl Liebknechts, a martyr of German Liberalism, is presented with the stark black and white linear manner of medieval German wood sculpture.

210.
Kasimir Malevich (Russian, 1878-1935)
CONGRESS OF COMMITTEES ON RURAL POVERTY
(front and back covers to the publication of the same name),
lithograph; edition: 10 or 12, 1918
h: 11 1/2 in, w: 11 1/2 in. (front cover);
h: 7 7/8 in., w: 7 7/8 in. (back cover)
The Art Museum League Fund
in honor of Mr. and Mrs. James H. Clark
1978.83.1-2

The Museum has a virtually complete collection of the graphics of the important Russian avant-garde artist Kasimir Malevich. In the last years of World War I, when Suprematist artists were producing designs for revolutionary posters or other political materials, Malevich designed this bookcover, for a text recording a committee meeting on rural poverty, in the dynamic abstract style of Suprematism.

211.
Frank Stella (American, born 1936)
INACCESSIBLE ISLAND RAIL, 35/50
1977
color lithograph and screenprint
h: 32 15/16 in., w: 44 13/16 in. (image);
h: 33 7/8 in., w: 45 13/16 in. (sheet)
Mr. and Mrs. Jake L. Hamon Fund
1977.76

Contemporary American artists have frequently been printmakers, as well as painters. To meet this creative need, the best fine arts presses are available to print their work, in what is now considered to be a major medium. Frank Stella's *Inaccessible Island Rail* is related in subject and style to the large mixed media wall reliefs he has been constructing in recent years.

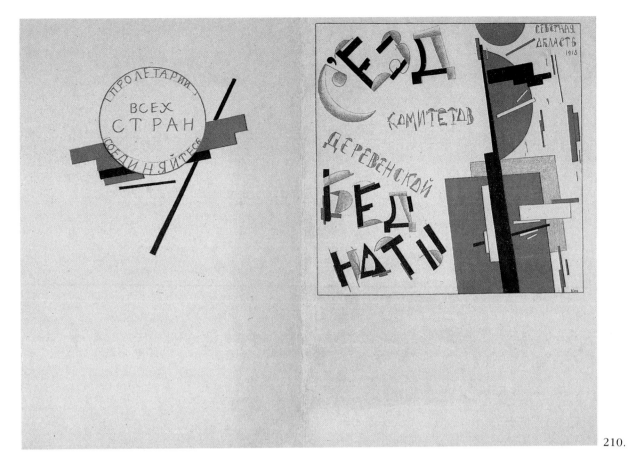

210.

Drawings

The Museum has a small collection of drawings, a few of which are related to larger works by the artists in the collections. The acquisition of drawings, both contemporary and historical, is an area in which the Museum hopes to expand its holdings.

212.
Eugène Delacroix (French, 1798-1863)
SHEET OF STUDIES FOR THE ''JUSTICE OF TRAJAN''
c.1840
pencil on paper
h: 8 11/16 in., w: 13 7/8 in.
Given in memory of Louie N. Bromberg and Mina Bromberg
by their sister Essie Bromberg Joseph
1982.40

An example of Old Master drawing is the sheet of studies by Eugène Delacroix for his large Salon painting of 1840, *The Justice of Trajan*. Delacroix is best known as a colorist and the originator of Romanticism in French art, but his masterly skill as a draughtsman may be seen in the rear view studies of a boy's figure, where forms are effortlessly and precisely defined.

213.
John Singer Sargent (American, 1856-1925)
STUDY FOR ''EL JALEO''
c.1880-1882
watercolor on paper
h: 12 in., w: 7 7/8 in.
Foundation for the Arts Collection,
gift of Mr. and Mrs. George V. Charlton
in memory of Eugene McDermott
1974.1.FA

John Singer Sargent was one of the finest American watercolorists, as well as a technically brilliant painter in oils. In 1882 Sargent displayed at the Paris Salon his most important early work, the large painting of a Spanish dancer, *El Jaleo*. This watercolor study for the main figure in the painting is very close to the final version, a dramatically lit female dancer, whose dress as well as pose suggest vibrant motion. Sargent's sparkling watercolor technique adds to the impression of exciting rhythm.

212.

13.

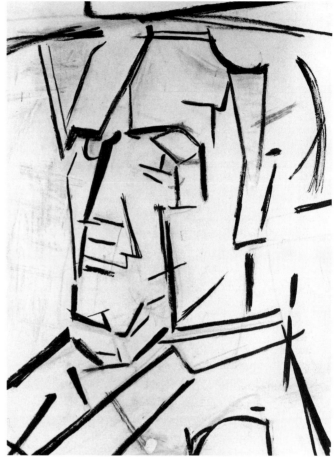

214.

214.
Piet Mondrian (Dutch, 1872-1944)
SELF-PORTRAIT
1942
ink and charcoal on paper with white heightening
h: 25 in., w: 19 in.
Foundation for the Arts Collection,
gift of the James H. and Lillian Clark Foundation
1982.23.FA

Piet Mondrian, as an abstract artist, was as much draughtsman as painter; the linear forms in his abstractions were defined by rulers and measures. This portrait of himself, the latest Mondrian created, is also a series of straight lines, but the slashing strokes convey a strong sense of Mondrian's appearance and personality. This drawing is a reworking of a self portrait Mondrian executed as far back as 1911.

216.

215.

215.
George Bellows (American, 1882-1925)
EMMA IN A PURPLE DRESS
1920
charcoal on paper
h: 14 in., w: 12 in.
Gift of H. V. Allison and Company
1960.124

216.
George Grosz (American, born Germany, 1893-1959)
PRO AND CONTRA
date unknown
ink on paper
h: 17 7/8 in., w: 23 in.
Dallas Art Association purchase
1949.8

George Bellows' important late portrait of his wife Emma is illustrated in Chapter 13. Bellows spent several years working on the portrait before he was finally satisfied with it. This preliminary drawing shows how easily he defined the luxurious dress, which forms such an important part of the rich, painterly impression made by the oil painting. It was the head and expression which Bellows continued to work and rework.

The Expressionist artist George Grosz came to America as an expatriate in 1932. His earlier work was political caricature and throughout his life he was concerned with the corruptions of a materialistic, capitalist society. Grosz's links with both Expressionism and Dada are apparent in the manic struggle of this scene, in which the middle classes seem engaged in frenzied self-destruction, reminiscent of W.H. Auden's line about "the brokers roaring like beasts on the floor of the Bourse".

Photographs

The Museum's photograph collection has centered on the work of living artists, but is beginning to expand into the area of historic masters of photography.

217.
Brassaï (Gyula Halasz), (French, born Transylvania, 1899)
MATISSE'S STUDIO FROM THE DOORWAY
negative: 1939, print: 1979
black and white photograph
h: 14 5/8 in., w: 11 1/16 in.
General Acquisitions Fund
1980.4

During the 1930s Brassaï (Gyula Halasz) photographed street scenes in Paris and views of the city at night, which turned the chaotic debris of a modern city into significant form. Later Brassaï, who was himself a sculptor and draughtsman, created a series on artists at work which have the same gift of unexpected vision. Henri Matisse is seen in his studio, with the flowers and nude model of his sensuous art, but the scene is framed by the doorway in such a way as to suggest Matisse is inside a painting.

218.
Minor White (American, 1908-1976)
GOLD ASSAY OFFICE, PORTLAND, OREGON
1940
black and white photograph
h: 13 1/2 in., w: 10 1/2 in.
Polaroid Foundation grant
1975.53

Minor White, an admirer of Edward Weston and Alfred Steiglitz, worked in their classical vein of formally pure photography. Through his teaching and his clearly defined, poetically resonant photographs, White has had considerable influence on later American work in the field. *Gold Assay Office, Portland, Oregon* is an example of the sharply defined, linear character of White's work, in which objects are given a living presence and power.

217.

218.

219.

219.
Laura Gilpin (American, 1891-1979)
SAN LUIS VALLEY AND SANGRE DE CRISTO
date unknown
black and white photograph
h: 30 in., w: 40 in.
Dallas Art Association purchase
1959.28

220.
Robert Mapplethorpe (American, born 1946)
UNTITLED (SEATED NUDE), 2/15
1981
black and white photograph
h: 19 3/4 in., w: 15 7/8 in.
General Acquisitions Fund
1981.99

The western photographer Laura Gilpin also produced work with great formal purity. Most of her photographs endeavor to penetrate the inner spirit of the American Southwest and the Indian life which was its human counterpart. The adobe forms of this building have a solid, earthy and timeless character. Georgia O'Keeffe painted similar subjects, but in contrast to her painterly abstraction, Gilpin's photograph has a sharp-edged clarity and stark chiaroscuro, which illustrates one possible use of the camera's eye.

Robert Mapplethorpe, a New York photographer, has done photographic work in a variety of styles. The Museum's photograph of a male nude, one of a series entitled *Black Males,* is again reminiscent of Edward Weston's experiments with formal compositions. The rounded, gleaming shapes of the man's body are strongly sculptural in effect. It is a study of compositional simplification and of light and texture, both elements of which form a brilliant unity.

221.
Geoff Winningham (American, born 1943)
OKLAHOMA BAND AT THE COTTON BOWL
1973; from the portfolio A TEXAS DOZEN, 12/15,
published 1976
black and white photograph
h: 16 in., w: 20 in.
Gift of Prestonwood National Bank
1981.36.7

In contrast with Mapplethorpe's photograph is the complex narrative scene by the Texas artist Geoff Winningham. It has a lively, completely momentary effect, though actually it captures some very relevant, even symbolic, aspects of modern life. The visiting college band at a football game is seen as funny, human, and slightly pathetic; behind them, the anonymous, cheering mass of spectators re-enact the yearly ritual of the Texas/O.U. game.

220.   221.

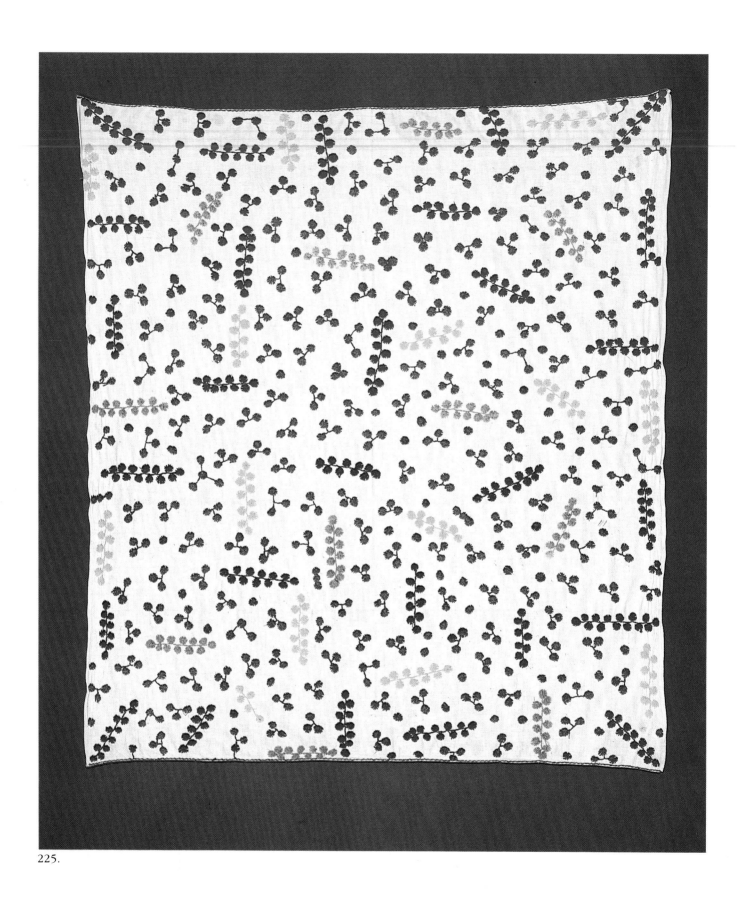

225.

XVII.

Textiles

Adjoining the Print and Drawing area is the Textile storage area, which serves a similar purpose. The Museum's textiles are available for scholarly study, while periodically there will be shows of historically important works in the exhibition room. The Nora and John Wise Collection of South American art includes many distinguished textiles, some of which are displayed in the Museum galleries, but most of which are stored in the study room. In addition, the Museum has other examples of textile art, which are displayed on a rotating basis.

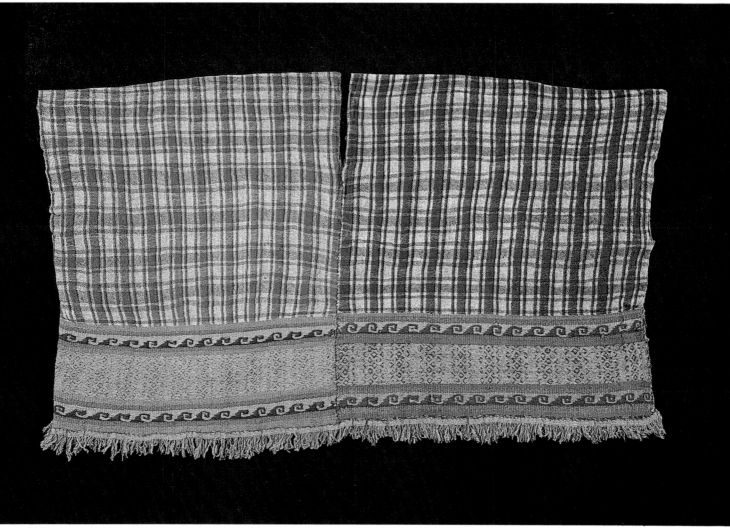

222.

223.

222.
TUNIC
Chimu style, c.A.D. 1350-1476
Peru: North Coast
plain weave with warp and weft stripes
  and supplementary-weft patterning; cotton
l: 20 1/4 in., w: 33 1/4 in.
The Nora and John Wise Collection,
gift of Mr. and Mrs. Jake L. Hamon,
the Eugene McDermott Family,
Mr. and Mrs. Algur H. Meadows
and the Meadows Foundation,
and Mr. and Mrs. John D. Murchison
1976.W1866

Peruvian textiles are remarkable for the wide range of techniques used in their manufacture. Indian weavers achieved an almost endless variety in their fabrics. This example from the North Coast Chimu culture has a bold plaid design in the natural brown, tan and cream colors of the cotton fiber from which it was woven. There are subtle contrasts between the plaid pattern and the running step-fret border, which encloses a very finely detailed strip of diamond patterning.

223.
TUNIC WITH ANIMAL MOTIF
Late Nasca style (Nasca 9), c.A.D. 600-700
Peru: South Coast
dovetailed tapestry weave; alpaca
l: 22 1/2 in., w: 30 1/4 in.
The Eugene and Margaret McDermott Fund
1970.20.McD

Contrasting with the subdued character of the Chimu tunic is the bright design of a late Nasca piece, with its glowing colors and angular feline patterns. Here, too, there is an interplay between large, simple forms and minute checkered design elements. The colors, derived from natural dyes, shift gradually in tone from one design unit to another, though the pattern remains the same. Such textiles would have been designed for people of high rank and were buried with them in their tombs.

224.
HUIPIL FOR THE FIGURE OF A SAINT
probably 1920s
Guatemala: department of Guatemala,
San Juan Sacatepequez (Cakchiquel Maya)
warp-faced plain weave with warp stripes
and supplementary-weft patterning; cotton and silk
l: 8 1/2 in., w: 11 3/4 in.
The Carolyn and Dan C. Williams Collection of Guatemalan Textiles,
gift of Carolyn and Dan C. Williams
1982.158

225. *illustration on page 208*
WOMAN'S HEADCLOTH (Tzut)
probably 1910-1930
Guatemala: department of Sacatepequez,
Magdalena Milpas Altas (Cakchiquel Maya)
embroidery on commercial plain weave: cotton
l: 38 in., w: 33 3/4 in.
The Carolyn and Dan C. Williams Collection of Guatemalan Textiles,
gift of Carolyn and Dan C. Williams
1982.170

The methods of Pre-Columbian weavers, including the use of a backstrap loom, cotton yarn and natural dyes, were handed down to their Indian descendants, among whom the techniques are still used today to make richly ornamental fabrics. In Guatemala, statues of Christian saints are decorated with elaborate clothes during church festivals. Some of the miniature garments are of wonderfully intricate manufacture and design, like this saint's huipil, which has a pattern of birds and animals and a rainbow of softly muted colors — white, aqua, yellow, lavender, purple and brown — on a rose-red ground.

There are other types of Guatemalan textile design besides the dense, overall pattern of the small huipil. A tzut, or woman's headcloth used for ceremonial occasions, has a very open pattern of widely scattered dot clusters. The bright field of red, green and yellow sprays on a cream ground is completely reversible. Such Guatemalan fabrics are generally made by women and are markedly localized in style, each village having its own characteristic patterns.

224.

228.

226.
SARONG
probably 1900-1920
Indonesia: Java, North Coast, probably Lasem
batik on commercial cotton
l: 80 1/4 in., w: 42 1/2 in.
Dallas Museum of Fine Arts purchase
1981.89

Time, patience and technical expertise are necessary for the creation of fine textiles. As in ceramic manufacture, the existence of a large demand for an art form leads to high production, variety, and experiment. In Indonesia, as in the Americas, a long tradition of sophisticated textile making meant a luxuriant richness of craftsmanship. This Javanese batik sarong, probably dating to the early 20th century, is composed of a diamond pattern, each segment of which encloses a different design. The inventive array of motifs, which includes plants, birds, flowers, bundles, insects and a spider web, shows Chinese influence. In the same way in which the design elements are highly varied within one pattern, the complex color combinations are created from a few primary dyes. It is this inventiveness in the design of batik dye patterns which gives Indonesian cotton batiks a richness that parallels work in rarer materials like silk.

226.

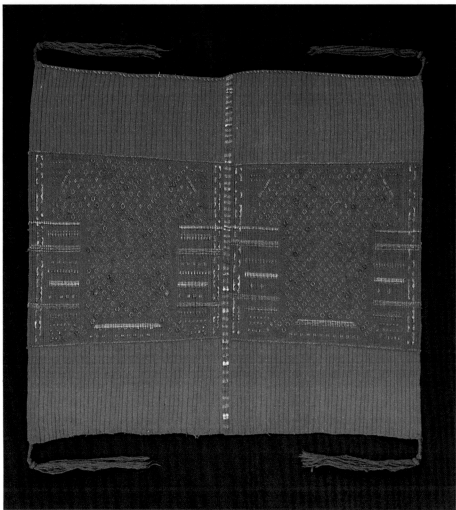

227.

227.
MAN'S HEADCLOTH (Tzut)
probably 1920-1935
Guatemala: department of Quiche,
Santa Tomas Chichicastenango
(Quiche Maya)
warp-faced plain weave with warp stripes and
supplementary-weft patterning; cotton and silk
l: 27 1/2 in., w: 30 1/4 in.
The Carolyn and Dan C. Williams Collection of Guatemalan Textiles,
gift of Carolyn and Dan C. Williams
1982.206

The complexity of design found in sophisticated textiles may be seen by comparing an early 20th century
Guatemalan man's tzut, or headcloth, with an Indonesian sarong. On the cotton tzut, a red ground at top
and bottom of the fabric is accentuated by dark blue
warp pin stripes. The wide central band has a purple
ground ornamented with designs in silk brocading.
Large double-headed bird figures, composed of diamond patterns, have contrasting small horizontal bar
elements on the wings and tail. This intricate patterning is given a three-dimensional accent by the bold
silk ornamentation of the central seam.

228.
SARONG (Lau pahudu padua)
Early 20th century
Indonesia: Sumba
warped-faced plain weave with warp *ikat*
and bands of supplementary-warp
l: 70 in., w: 25 in.
General Acquisitions Fund
1981.16

An Indonesian woman's sarong from Sumba displays
an equally subtle interplay of elements. Central bands
with woven geometric designs are flanked by softer
toned bands in the *ikat* technique, where the warp
threads are dyed in the desired pattern before weaving.
In turn, these wide contrasting bands are flanked by
plain dark bands and by diamond patterned border
stripes. The rust, cream and dark blue colors of the
fabric were supplemented by brown areas painted on
after the cloth was woven, giving the textile an under-
stated richness.

Edward Larrabee Barnes & Associates
New Dallas Museum of Art: *Front Elevation*
1982
pencil on paper
h: 25 7/16 in., w: 53 3/8 in.
Gift of Edward Larrabee Barnes & Associates
1982.145

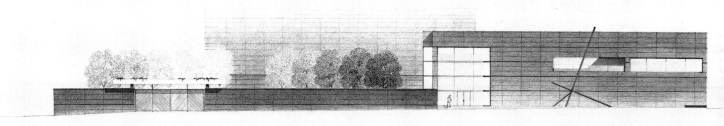

Edward Larrabee Barnes & Associates
New Dallas Museum of Art:
Front — exterior view of facade
1982
pen on paper
h: 25 7/16 in., w: 89 1/2 in.
Gift of Edward Larrabee Barnes & Associates
1982.147

Architect's Statement

The new home for the Dallas Museum of Art will be in the inner ring of Dallas, slated to become an "arts district," with museum, symphony hall, and opera house all within walking distance of each other. Despite the downtown setting with high buildings rising all around, this is essentially a low-rise structure with garden courts and patios and top-lighted galleries.

The museum has three entrances, connected by a "spine" hallway gently ramping down the sloping site and providing access to the various activities as well as to the main galleries. All the activities can be opened or closed on their own schedules, like shops on a street.

It is the galleries of the permanent collection that set the tone of the whole museum. They are arranged on three levels, each with its own character. First, there are the contemporary galleries — cruciform space embracing four box-like rooms. A 45-foot-high white plastered vault crosses the axis of the vista toward the Sculpture Garden.

The next level contains the collection of European and American art, a serene space with daylighted outer walls, Miesian screens, and a central patio with a wisteria vine and a quiet pool. The third level contains objects in cases and also has some daylighted walls and a patio, here shaded with yaupon holly. The exit from the third level leads back to the "spine" by way of a grand cascade stair.

The terracing of the museum on three levels gives coherence to the diverse collections. The visitor may progress in either direction, from the bottom up or, chronologically, from the top down, starting with ethnic and ancient art, down through our European heritage, through contemporary work and out to the Sculpture Garden. When the museum expands over the parking area, two more terraces will be added; visitors will take an escalator to the very top and slowly descend five levels back to the entrance.

Flow is as important as form. Certainly progression through a museum has elements of ceremony. There must be a sense of entrance, of logical sequence, of climax, and return. And this progression must be closely related to the art on display. The museum is an architectural composition involving time — the measured unfolding of the collection in quiet, supportive space.

What kind of architecture supports art rather than competes with it? Obviously highly sculptural or overbearing architecture can upstage the art on display. At the same time, anonymous loft space with no relief of any kind can be monotonous. The theory of the Dallas design is that soft, indirect daylight and splashes of daylight from windows and garden courts and patios enchance the works. This kind of punctuation provides a counterpoint by relating art to nature.

Otherwise the architecture is very quiet. The entire exterior including the vault roof is limestone, cut in huge blocks, coursed with deep V-cuts to set off the stepping of the mass.

Edward Larrabee Barnes
1982

Staff

OFFICE OF THE DIRECTOR

Harry S. Parker III
Director

Lawrence Francell
Coordinator, New Museum

Ann Smith
Administrative Assistant to the Director

Robert V. Rozelle
Publisher/Publicity Director

Joan McClendon
Publicity Assistant

Anne R. Bromberg
Curator for Education

Roberta Mathews
Associate Curator for Education

Ellen Methner
Assistant Curator for Education-Outreach

Melissa Berry
Administrative Assistant

Joyce Hagen-Brenner
Education Assistant

Dorothy Taliaferro
Assistant for Outreach

Mary H. Mills
Administrator, Visual Resources

Edith Riley
Assistant, Visual Resources

CURATORIAL

Steven A. Nash
Assistant Director/Chief Curator

John Lunsford
Senior Curator

Sue Graze
Curator for Contemporary Art

Carol Robbins
Associate Curator

Ginger Geyer
Assistant Curator, Special Projects

Vicki Vinson
Assistant for Collection Management

Anne Umland
Administrative Assistant

Jacqueline Gilliam
Adjunct Conservator

Jo Anne Griffin
Adjunct Conservator

David Wharton
Adjunct Photographer

Barney Delabano
Curator for Exhibitions

Anna McFarland
Assistant Curator for Exhibitions

Manuel Mauricio
Gallery Technician

Russell Sublette
Gallery Technician

Mark Snedegar
Gallery Technician

Esther Houseman
Exhibitions Assistant

Larry Harmon
Carpenter/Packer

Debra Richards
Registrar

Ann Fricke
Assistant Registrar

Donna Rhein
Librarian

Amy Giesler
Assistant Librarian

PUBLIC AFFAIRS

Carolyn B. Foxworth
Assistant Director for Public Relations

Ryland S. Stacy
Associates Membership Director

Pamela Maedgen
Corporate Membership Director

Petrine Abrahams
Development Assistant

Beth Beran
League Secretary/Volunteer Coordinator

Jane Simpson
Director of Membership

Marilyn Franklin
Computer Operator

Jeri Harris
Membership Assistant

Linda Miller
Membership Assistant

ADMINISTRATION

Thomas A. Livesay
Assistant Director for Administration

Susan Adams
Assistant for Administration

Cassondra Armstrong
Receptionist

Lee Breeden
Comptroller

June Browning
Head Bookkeeper

Patsy Harris
Supervisor of Accounts

Cathy Jones
New Museum Bookkeeper

Gene Thompson
Museum Shop Manager

Kay Rath
Museum Shop Assistant Manager

Janet Balch
Shop Assistant

Anne Mason
Shop Assistant

Sally Lewellyn
Shop Assistant

Nancy Wallof
Gallery Buffet Manager

Helen Brooks
Jean Jackson
Shirley Green
Kenneth Bryant
Gallery Buffet Staff

Lonnie Carter
Shipping/Receiving

E. J. Carter
Head Porter

Herbert Deckard
Robert Hopkins
Louis Mentor
Willie Jackson
Alberta McGowan
Maintenance Staff

Tom Linthicum
Chief of Security

Johnny Fertitta
Ray Clement
Head Guards

Ben Blair
Gabriel Brisco
Otto Carwile
Ray Coleman
Alvin Donahoo
David Dozier
William Jackson
Edward Lacy
Harry Legget
Frances Leyenberger
George Meusel
William Rohrbach
Tim Royal
Joe Sanders
Tom Scallorn
Mack Turrentin
Edward Wimpee
Guards

Museum Services

In addition to its stewardship of the City's art collections, the Dallas Museum of Art provides a broad range of educational services for the community. The Education Department organizes daily tours by trained docents for schoolchildren and adults; it also schedules special events, including regular series of lectures, films, and concerts. The Education Wing, funded and staffed, in part, by the Junior League of Dallas, offers programs designed especially for children in a unique educational environment. The Study Room is available as a scholarly resource for the community, and is adjacent to the Museum's collections of textiles, prints, drawings, and photographs. The Museum's volunteer service organization, the DMA League, provides staff support for the information desks, shops, libraries, and Gallery Buffet restaurant.

Daniel Barsotti